Covenant Renewal
In Religious Life

Covenant Renewal In Religious Life

BIBLICAL REFLECTIONS

by
Stephen C. Doyle O.F.M.

FRANCISCAN HERALD PRESS

1434 WEST 51st STREET • CHICAGO, 60609

Convenant Renewal in Religious Life: Biblical Reflections by Stephen C. Doyle O.F.M. Copyright ©1975 by Franciscan Herald Press, 1434 West 51st Street, Chicago, Illinois 60609

Library of Congress Cataloging in Publication Data

Doyle, Stephen C
  Covenant renewal in religious life.

  Bibliography: p.
  Includes index.
  1. Monastic and religious life. 2. Spiritual life—
Biblical teaching. I. Title.
BX2435.D68   248'.894   75-19394
ISBN 0-8199-0585-2

NIHIL OBSTAT:
  MARK HEGENER O.F.M.
  Censor

IMPRIMATUR:
  MSGR. RICHARD A. ROSEMEYER, J.D.
  Vicar General, Archdiocese of Chicago

MADE IN THE UNITED STATES OF AMERICA

Since you have accepted Jesus Christ
    as Lord
Sink your roots deep in him
    grow ever stronger in the Faith
    and be filled with thanksgiving.

Eph 2:6, 7

Foreword

"The Religious state reveals in a unique way that the kingdom of God and its overmastering necessities are superior to all earthly considerations . . . To all men it shows wonderfully at work within the Church the surpassing greatness of the force of Christ the King and the boundless power of the Holy Spirit." (*Dogmatic Constitution on the Church,* par. 44) Thus, did the Fathers of the Second Vatican Council describe religious life as a microcosm of the life of the Church, which they, in turn, called "a kind of sacrament or sign of intimate union with God, and of the unity of all mankind." (*Ibid.,* par. 1)

Religious life may also be looked upon in the analogy of a sacrament. The common life is an external manifestation, the outward sign, of an inner reality. That inner reality is the unity, the community, which Christ our Lord accomplishes in making us one in mind and heart with him. Since Vatican II, great efforts have been and are continuing to be made to update and adapt the outward forms, structures, and constitutions of religious life in accordance with the life and mission of the Church. These efforts, precisely because we are a pilgrim church, have not been achieved without some measure of individual resistance and personal pain that usually accompany all authentic growth.

The Fathers explained that renewal involves much more than the mere adaptation or modification of the outward forms of religious life. It involves "two simultaneous processes: a continuous return to the sources of all Christian life and to the original inspiration behind a given community, and an adjustment to the Community to the changed conditions of the times." (*Decree on the Renewal of Religious Life*, par. 2) The Fathers particularly pleaded for a true renewal of the inner reality of each religious community, for a "renewal of spirit" that gives life to them, for a renewal that leads those who embrace religious life to a closer imitation of Christ and to a deeper union with God. They urged all members of religious communities earnestly to cultivate a spirit and practice of prayer: "In the first place they whould take the sacred Scriptures in hand each day by way of attaining 'the excelling knowledge of Jesus Christ' (Phil. 3:8) through reading these divine writings and meditating on them." (*Ibid.*, par. 6)

The author of this book is eminently able to help religious men and women, and all lovers of the Lord, to become more deeply "rooted in Him and built on Him" (Col. 2:7), so that we may live our whole life according to the Christ we all received. Father Doyle is himself a dedicated religious priest, a most competent scriptural scholar and professor, an international lecturer and publisher, and a most refreshing human being. His own life bespeaks what he so successfully seeks to promote by this book: to help religious, and others, find their identity in God's own Word!

+Humberto Cardinal Medeiros
Archbishop of Boston

Contents

Introduction

The decree on the appropriate renewal of religious life of the second Vatican Council has indicated that aggiornamento in religious orders and congregations will be achieved by paying close attention to three criteria. The first is a "continuous return to the sources of all Christian life," the Scriptures; the second is a return to the spirit which brought the community into being; and the third is a reading of the signs of the times, or "a suitable awareness of contemporary human conditions and of the needs of the Church."

This book is intended to concern itself with renewal through the Word of God. But this must be seen in the context of the second and third criteria. The effort to return to the charism of the founder, or the spirit which brought a community into being will be as varied as there are orders and congregations in the Church. By an honest remembering where they came from, communities will be able to discern how it came to be that the original charism was able to flourish and to have been such a gift to the Church. Then, with a realism that excludes a false historicism of trying to mimic the founder, they will be able to discover how the varied, but no less genuine charism of the community and each individual member may flourish in the Church today. There will never be another Mother Seton, Ignatius Loyola, Catherine McCauley, Francis of Assisi, or Charles de Foucald. But unless their followers search out what it was that caused them to be what they were, they will wander aimlessly and without roots.

The third criterion, reading the signs of the times, demands that, enriched by our knowledge of the past, we nevertheless refuse to be museum keepers. We know where we have been in the past, not in a vain effort to repeat it, but that we might be more alive in the present. To read the signs of the times, is to do no more than the founders did in their own times. It is to recognize that communities, as well as the Church and world that they were founded to serve, have grown and progressed from the age in which the founders so well recognized the signs of their own times. It is a refusal to be custodians of anachronistic customs and costumes under guise of fidelity to the past. At the same time it demands a posture of listening. What are the times saying? What are the needs of the present that are crying out for help? What are they asking of us?

Such a criterion demands that we live fully in the twentieth century at the same time as we respond to the condition of those for whom life is less than full in the twentieth century. Jesus, a man of his times, read well the signs of the times when he perceived that the people were like sheep without a shepherd.

And so, by what he was, and what he did, he gave them life, hope and vision.

This criterion, so easily abused and exaggerated when used independently of the other two, is absolutely necessary if we are not to appear like people setting up deck chairs on the Titanic. The fact that some will set off in hot pursuit of every fad, identifying their own breathlessness with the breath of the Spirit is no excuse for paralysis. Inactivity, bred of fear of abuse and making mistakes is a death wish. It has been said that the seven last words of religious life are: "We never did it that way before."

The goal to be achieved by this third criterion was well stated in a letter of Pope Paul VI to the General Chapter of the Friars Minor.

People do not ask of you, that you harmonize with the world in an equivocal fashion; for they are demanding that you show forth to them the sublimity of your own way of life, so that by looking upon it they may begin to have qualms about their own lives and may seek the city to come (cf. Hdb 13:14). Even at this time men are searching their souls for something absolute, which transcends nature; even at this time they can be led on to God by all created realities which have been reconciled through Christ (cf. Col 1:19ff) and which speak of God. Saint Francis gave your own spirituality this special mark and characteristic: it was to show that the world could be transformed in such a way that work could be called a grace, and death a sister.-

But the first criterion for the renewal of religious life is a return to the Scriptures. As the Council states: "Since the fundamental norm of all religious life is a following of Christ as proposed by the Gospel, such is to be regarded by all communities as their supreme law." The Word of God must form the backbone of our spirituality, and our attempts to discern spirits and search out the will of God today. Only through continuous comparision of our life and efforts with the invitation and challenge that the Word offers, will we know that our efforts are truly his.

The Council's call for a *continuous* return to the Scriptures is hardly satisfied by lacing new constitutions with Biblical quotes. Nor is it sufficient to provide Scripture workshops, as helpful as they may be for a beginning. Each community, and each member must be thoroughly imbued, in prayer, in chapter, in community and in apostolate with God's creative Word. If we are to claim with any seriousness that the religious vocation is a call from Jesus Christ, then the words of St. Jerome must strike into our hearts. "For ignorance of the Scriptures is ignorance of Christ."

The return to the Scriptures is not without difficulty. As Christians who have been accustomed to found our spirituality on things other than the Bible, "The continuous return to the sources of all Christian life," the Scriptures, will demand a re-orientation if not a conversion. But it was no less a conversion that was demanded of Paul who had centered his spirituality on what he thought would make him holy. "But those things I used to consider gain I have now reappraised as loss in the light of Christ. I have come to rate all as loss in the light of the surpassing knowledge of my Lord Jesus Christ" (Phil 3:7).

Added to this challenge of rediscovering the sources

of our spirituality are the fears engendered in the non-scholar by the major leaps that have been made in Biblical studies in recent years. But, when followed with a little effort, these strides in Biblical scholarship will be seen to have no other purpose than to allow the communication of God's Word to come through more clearly.

It is precisely in the hope that these difficulties can be overcome that this book on the Biblical background of the major themes of religious life is offered. It has one purpose: That with the power of the Spirit who first inspired the Word, religious today may become men and women of the Word. The first community called by God was told that they would be a community insofar as they "hearken to my voice." (Ex 19:5). The times have changed and their signs must be read, the founders are with the Lord, and their charisms must inspire our own, but there is still no way to be a community, except to "hearken to his voice."

The Gospels were written by men who gave their name to books which were in reality the concretization of a vision of the Good News that had been shared with them by the Christian community. I put my name as the author of these chapters in the same way. They are a result of a vision shared by the communities in which I have lived, and the communities with whom I have broken the bread of God's Word.

Stephen C. Doyle, O.F.M.
Rome, the Feast of the Annunciation
Holy Year, 1975

NOTE

The themes treated in this book are of interest to all Christians, not just religious. However, they have been suggested by many religious as the areas which are of most concern to them today. The number chosen was limited by both the format and purpose of the book.

It can be used by individuals for reading and meditation on the Bible. It can also be used as a resource and basis for community sharing and discussion. Its twenty-four short chapters could be used for monthly meetings over a two year period, or every other week for one year.

It should be noted, however, that this book is concerned with Biblical roots, and not later developments in religious life. The term "community" is used neither to canonize nor criticize either large or small groupings, liberals or conservatives, or open or closed communities. Such distinctions as much as they may reflect legitimate growth and experimentation, are not Biblical. Community here is used only in the Biblical sense, and that has many manifestations: Abraham and his nomad family, Paul on the road alone or with one or two, the "Sons of the prophets," Jesus and the Apostles, as well as the local churches. They were all trying to live out what God had accomplished: covenant community.

1.

CALL TO COVENANT

Each of us no doubt has a Bible. It is widely disseminated by groups founded to spread it throughout the world. It is known to be the best-seller of all time. There are millions of Bibles in existence in practically every known language. But, because it has become so common, it may be in danger of becoming commonplace. We can easily take for granted that there should be a Bible.

To appreciate it for what it is, we ought really to stand back and be amazed that there is such a book at all. God did not have to speak. We have no right that obligates him to speak even one word. We can make no demand that he reveal himself and his will.

Yet, fantastically enough, he has spoken. We do have the Bible. Why? Why should there be a Bible at all? What is the reason for its existence?

The Bible is different from any other book ever written, and in that difference lies the answer to our questions. Other books impart information, give advice, entertain, instruct or share knowledge. The Bible alone was written as an invitation. It is revelation, not only in the sense of the uncovering hidden facts, but in revealing a God who is love, and from that love calls, invites and cajoles his creatures to do what he does: love.

1

The response to other books may be intellectual stimulation or interest, but the Bible is an invitation with an RSVP. It is the only book that demands a radical yes or no to its invitation.

The very names that we have given to our divisions of the Bible tell us what it is about. It is Old Testament and New Testament, or better, Old Covenant and New Covenant. Covenant is the bond of unity which God holds out to man. It is life with him, never again to be alone or in isolation. The constant refrain through the Old Testament is the statement and affirmation of covenant: "I will be your God, you will be my people."

The very meaning of his name, revealed in the call of Moses at the burning bush (Ex 4), is that HE IS who is with us, who will guide us and give us life and salvation.

But this life is not just one on one. We are his people. Covenant is community. Community is the ultimate reality, which God himself is, and what he calls us to be, with himself and each other.

Today we frequently hear of an identity crisis in religious life. It is not new. From the time when the Israelites accepted the invitation of his Word through Moses, the Israelites had such an identity crisis. Freed from the slavery of Egypt, they wanted to know what God wanted of them. What was he calling them to be and to do?

Even before Moses gave them the commandments, telling them what to do, he came to the rescue of their identity crisis and told them what Yahweh wanted them to be. In Exodus 19, the Lord sends Moses down from the mountain with these words:

Therefore, if you hearken to my voice and keep my covenant, you shall be my special possession, dearer to me than all other people, though all the earth is mine. You shall be to me a kingdom of priests, a holy nation.

Before they were to do anything, they were, as a result of listening to his Word, and responding to his covenant love, to be a community, a kingdom, a nation. But they were to be a community with a difference. They were to be a community that is taken up into his holiness. They are a community set apart in the mystery of him who is wholly 'other.' Still they were not to remain apart, for by being his holy community they would be priestly mediators and revealers of his holiness to all mankind. By the very fact of being taken up into the mystery of his life and love, by being community, they would have a priestly function for all of mankind. Thus does God show them that community is the ultimate reality, and the source of their own identity. They will come to realize who he is, and who they are by being community. The Israelites, by being the community that he called them to be, by saying yes to covenant, would, by that very fact, be a sign of the reality of God, and the reality of his call, in a world which was oblivious of him. What are they to do? They are to be! He shows them that to live in covenanted community with him and each other, is itself a sign and an apostolate, without which every other activity will fail for it will be merely human effort.

Jesus clarified it even further for the tiny community of his first followers. "Such as my love has been for you so must your love be for one another. This is how all will know you for my disciples, your love for one another" (Jn 13:34). The reality of Jesus will come to be known because of a community of love.

If community is the end and purpose of the Bible, it is the end and purpose of the Incarnation itself. The Biblical Word is a call to community, and so is the Word made Flesh. "Any who did accept him he empowered to become children of God" (Jn 1:12).

Later on, meditating toward the end of his life, Paul finds that the very reason for the existence of the universe is community in Jesus Christ.

God chose us in him before the world began, to be holy and blameless in his sight, to be full of love; he likewise predestined us through Christ Jesus to be his adopted sons—such was his will and pleasure (Eph 1:12).

If we may speak this way, the Father thought of Christ and community before he thought of creation.

At the end of his life Jesus reveals that community is the very reason for the existence of the Church.

I do not pray for them alone. I pray also for those who will believe in me through their word, that all may be one as you Father, are in me, and I in you; I pray that they may be one in us that the world may believe that you sent me (Jn 17:20,21).

The reason for revelation, incarnation, redemption, creation, as well as the new creation which is the Church, is community. There can be no other reason for the existence of religious life. Before we *do* anything, God has called us to *be* his people.

Yet, if we have much difficulty in trying to define this community into which he has called us, it is no surprise. It is a mystery, like love, and if we can define love, it is pretty certain that we have never been in it. We can no more tie up community in a neat definition, than we can tie up God in a neat definition. But because it cannot be defined, does not mean it cannot be achieved.

But we must beware of thinking that we ourselves can achieve it. The statement so frequently heard of efforts to form community, is literally blasphemous. Forming community is God's work, not man's. We can only hearken to his voice, learn what he has accomplished in us, and then let our lives show forth what he has done.

2.

SIGNS OF THE CALL
_____ FOR ALL MANKIND

While the Lord has spoken his call to covenant to all mankind there are many who have not yet heard it, or not yet responded. Still, he never ceases to call, not only through his Word, but also in the lives of those who have already said "yes" to life with him in covenant. Their lives will speak to all mankind of his call. Their lives are to be an invitation to those who have not heard, to come and experience the love of the living God. "Your life may be the only Gospel some people will ever read," is not a modern cliche on a banner. It is the very essence of the Biblical vocation to covenant life with God.

This is what it means to be a "Chosen People." The choice is not because God has good taste, but because he has a role for his people in his plan to call all mankind.

Abraham, our father in faith (Roman Canon), received a vocation that manifests clearly that life in covenant is itself an apostolate.

I will make of you a great nation, and I will bless you; I will make your name great, so that you will be a blessing. I will bless those who bless you and curse those who curse you. All the communities of the earth shall find blessing in you (Gn· 12:2,3).

7

Abraham's faith, life and response are to be a source of blessing not just upon himself and a few acres of Mesopotamia. His life in covenant was a blessing on no less than all of mankind. The Biblical concept of blessing is that the blessed one is so manifestly touched by God that God's power, concern, love, and indeed his very existence are shown forth to others through this person. This is done not by any fantastic and amazing signs other than the fantastic and amazing sign of life with God in covenant. In a life of response to God's call, all mankind will be blessed, for in that life they will hear their own call to covenant.

No story was included in the Biblical text to satisfy curiosity. Abraham's vocation, so important that it was narrated three times, like three gospels proclaiming the same event (Gn 12,15,17), is no exception. The later generations which wrote it down, did so because they knew that his vocation must be their own. It was done to show the entire community of Israel what kind of response to covenant they must have, and what would be the result. "All the communities of the earth shall find blessing in you" (Gn 12:3).

Moses reaffirmed this (Ex 19:4-8) when he informed the Israelites that being God's special possession implied being a priestly people. The life of all the people in covenant community would have a priestly, a mediating effect on others. Their call was not just for themselves but for all of mankind.

This ideal, that vocation to covenant community is by its very nature an apostolate, became rather obscured in the course of Israel's history. Introspection and nationalism as well as the danger of being absorbed by the surrounding nations put her on the defensive. All too often she became more concerned to be a powerful kingdom than a kingdom of priests by the power of God.

However, their later meditation upon the vocation of Abraham shows that the ideal was never totally eclipsed. Also, from time to time powerful prophetic voices atten ted to waken them from their self-complacency. Such prophets tried to make them understand that being chosen meant little, if they forgot why they were chosen. It was for responsibility, not privilege. In the eighth century Amos scolded them:

You alone have I favored, more than all the families of the earth; Therefore I will punish you for all your crimes (Am 3:2).

They were not living out the call so that others might hear. They were more responsible than those who had not heard his voice. Indeed their lives were a countersign that muted his voice and raised static in his communication to all the communities of the earth who were supposed to find blessings in Israel.

Two hundred years later the catastrophe of the exile brought down upon their heads the result of their own narrow, selfish vision. But even in that devastating period the voice of an anonymous prophet, whose message was joined to Isaiah (hence called Deutero or second Isaiah), was raised to proclaim Israel's vocation. He speaks of the role of the servant, at once the corporate personality of Israel (Is 49:3) and an individual who is the personification of her vocation (Is

49:6a). "I will make you a light to the nations, that my salvation may reach to the ends of the earth" (Is 49:6b).

However, her near extinction in the exile caused Israel to turn further in on herself. Even the humorous story of Jonah, who thought that God could love only Israelites, was meant to get people to stop taking themselves so seriously and to get them to laugh at their own narrow-mindedness.

In addition to these voices of individuals, there arose also communities of witness within the larger covenant community. While it would be an anachronism to search out religious community life in the Bible, these communities, living a life of strict fidelity to the covenant as a witness to the larger community, do provide an analogy. The disciples or "sons" of the prophets (Is 8:16), the Nazirites (Am 2:11), the Rechabites (Jer 35:2), and the fascinating community of Qumran, seem to have been communities within the community. They spoke with a collective voice of the meaning of Israel's vocation. Recognizing the hopelessness of their own times when the words of the prophets had fallen upon deaf ears they preserved those words and passed them on with the hope of a community to come who would listen and respond.

That Jesus perceived himself to be the successor to those prophetic voices is evident from his first preaching in Luke.

When the book of the prophet Isaiah was handed him, he unrolled the scroll and found the passage where it was written: "The spirit of the Lord is upon me; therefore he has anointed

me. He has sent me to bring glad tidings to the poor, to proclaim liberty to captives, recovery of sight to the blind and release to prisoners, to announce a year of favor from the Lord."
Rolling up the scroll he gave it back to the assistant and sat
down. All in the synagogue had their eyes fixed on him. Then
he began by saying to them, "Today this Scripture, passage
is fulfilled in your hearing" (Lk 4:17–21).

This is soon followed by the call of the first disciples, the community within the community of Israel.
And if Israel had forgotten its vocation, Jesus did not.
"You are the salt of the earth. . . . You are the light
of the world" (Mt 5:13, 14).

It would be erroneous to identify one group of
Christians, such as religious, with discipleship, since
all men are called to that (Mt 28:19). It is evident
however that discipleship can be and is in the gospels manifested by many different life styles. Zachaeus,
giving up but half his wealth, and Martha, Mary and
Lazarus with their home, certainly lived a life style
different from those who were told to provide themselves with neither gold nor silver nor traveling bag
nor sandals (Mt 10:9,10). But whatever their life style,
they were called to be the light of the world, witnesses of the call for each other and all mankind. This
was true whether of the communal life of the Jerusalem church, idealized by Luke in Acts 4:32 ff., or
the rugged individualism of Paul who was a light to
so many communities.

Today's discussions concerning the relative priority
of community and apostolate find little basis in Scripture. Life in covenant must always be an apostolate.
Life in community is nothing if it does not speak to

the larger community and to all mankind of the reality of God, his love and his call. Life in community is a charism at the service of the entire community, showing in a special way what God can do. Like Abraham, communities are to show forth God's blessing and in that very life, the voice of the living God will cry out so that all may be his people and he may be their God.

3.

CHARISM AT THE SERVICE
_____OF THE CHURCH

A charism, by its very definition and derivation is a gift, freely given and unmerited. Unfortunately it is one of those words that has not gone untainted by its adoption into English. It has little to do with the magnetic power of politicians to attract votes by knowing when to kiss babies. It stems from the same root as charity, or unselfish love. The same root, *"charis"*, is usually translated as grace. Every gift of God, but especially the call to covenant life, is a charism.

In addition to the fact that the recipient can do nothing to merit or demand a charism, it is never given to isolate him from his community or to raise him to a superior or privileged place above the community. Charismata are given for no other reason than the service of the community.

There are different gifts (charismata) but the same Spirit; there are different ministries but the same Lord; there are different works but the same God who accomplishes all of them in everyone. To each person the manifestation of the Spirit is given for the common good (I Cor 12:4-7).

Every other charism must have life in the covenant community as its foundation, a life which implies building up and serving that community. If individuals or smaller communities within the community are given other charismata, it is never to make them superior, but rather servants of the community. Charismata never create elite groups, "super-communities".

Rather than a sense of privilege a charism usually causes fear and trembling. Exodus 3 and 4 show the surprise, awe and reluctance of Moses as he disputes with God about the charism of serving his people as their leader. He would readily have sent Yahweh to another employment agency to find someone more suitable and gifted. But that acknowledgement of weakness was precisely Yahweh's point. He chooses the most unlikely candidates to show that it is his gift 'at work, not their power.

Unfortunately the abuse of charismata for self-aggrandizement becomes more the rule than the exception in the Old Testament. Kingship and priesthood, both gifts to a community that needed structure, came to be looked upon as prizes. Service to the community was turned into social climbing above it.

Samuel's description of how the kings would act (I Sm 8), is an all too accurate picture of what happened when men, given the charism of being the superior *of* the community, took it to mean that they were superior *to* the community.

The clergy fared no better. Given the charism of imparting torah, the Lord's will, and leading the community in the celebration of their covenant life in sign, they soon preferred to be occupied with their stipends. Since they got the choice cuts from the sacrifices they inclined toward convincing the people that more was better. Multiplying sacrifices would keep God on their side (and the priests well fed!).

Put on a pedestal by the people, they found it more comfortable to be there with assurance of being served double lamb chops, than using their charism to serve the people. As was said of the early Protestant missionaries in the South Pacific, they came to do good, and they did well!

Hosea's charismatic voice of prophecy rises in protest against this abuse of the priestly charism:

My people perish for want of knowledge! Since you have rejected knowledge, I will reject you from my priesthood (Hos 4:6).

It seems ever to be the occupational hazard of individuals or groups with a special charism within the covenant community to develop a superiority complex. Too readily do they begin to consider themselves as a specially endowed and elite group over and above what they begin to think of as—the common herd.

The apostles themselves were not immune to the temptation. Their desire for the first place is narrated in all four gospels and twice in Luke. The second time, as if to highlight the insidiousness of it, Luke places it in the context of the Last Supper, shortly after the words of consecration (Lk 22:24). Jesus had to remind them, even at that sacred moment when he was giving his Body and Blood for them, that their charism as apostles was precisely for the service of the community. John emphasizes the point further by omitting the institution of the Eucharist at the last supper and presenting the washing of the feet as the sign of giving that must be imitated.

Do you understand what I just did for you? You address me as 'Teacher' and 'Lord,' and fittingly enough, for that is what I am. But if I washed your feet—I who am Teacher and Lord—then you must wash each other's feet. What I just did was to give you an example: as I have done, so you must do (Jn 13:13-15).

And yet not too long after this startling witness of the meaning of charism Paul found the ugliest abuses in the community of Corinth. Aware of the richness of the charismata they have received (I Cor 1:4 ff.) Paul is shocked at how they are used. The entire letter reflects a situation of fragmentation, polarization and elitism. The whole can be covered by the umbrella of gnosticism. This was a heresy of those who claim to have the charism of special knowledge (gnosis) that gives rise to an elite spirituality with special access to God, thus dividing the community into the "super-Christians" and the hoi poloi.

While Paul is reluctant to deny that any charism is an authentic gift of the Spirit, he strongly denies that such gifts have any other purpose than the service of the community. Even when viewing his own charism of celibate life as an apostle, he sees it as a gift for service, not privileged position placing him above those who are given other charismata. In reference to marriage he says: "Each one has his own gift (charism) from God, one this and another that" (I Cor 7:7).

No matter what the charism, there are no "super-Christians" in the Church, but all have gifts to build up the community. "To each person the manifestation of the Spirit is given for the common good" (I Cor

12:7).

If we may call religious life a charism, and popes and councils frequently have, then it has the same functions and pitfalls of the other charismata. It must be a manifestation of the vibrant presence of the Spirit to the whole Church. It must be a life of service to the community, a visible witness of the role of the servant Church to all mankind. And since charismata never divide, religious life must be a sign of the unity for which Christ prayed and which Paul knew no better way to describe than to say that in Christ we are more closely related than the finger is to the hand.

Since charismata never set the recipients apart from the pilgrim community in a privileged position, implying a superior spirituality, religious life will not have arisen above the gnosticism condemned by Paul if it gives such an impression. It is a charism not of superiority but of service.

4.

_____HEARERS OF THE WORD

The first chapter of the Bible, the priestly account of creation in Genesis I, was one of the latest chapters actually to be written down. In the sixth century, the priests in exile in Babylon, far away from the ruins of the Jerusalem temple and unable to have a liturgical function, returned finally to their original charism of listening to the Word and imparting God's will.

The situation in Babylon was critical for the faith of the people of the covenant. Each New Year's day the pagan priests honored Marduk, god of Babylon, with a magnificent celebration of his role as creator of the world. The Jews standing on the sidelines of the great processional street heard the Enuma Elish, the great epic of creation. On this, the first day of the new year, which contained a promise of continuing creation, they heard how Marduk, Babylon's own protector, had emerged victorious from a battle among the gods and created the world from the corpses of the vanquished (who just happened to be his parents!).

Already discouraged by their own exile and the destruction of the city of David and the house of their God, the Jews began to think that maybe the Babylonians were right. Maybe they had been foolish in putting all their eggs in one basket, Yahweh's. Did not their own defeat by the Babylonians indicate that their God had been vanquished by Marduk?

Sensing this crisis of faith, and realizing that Judea had been brought to its knees, not because Yahweh was weak, but because the people had ceased to listen to his Word, the priests produced their own account of creation.

Countering the pagan version, they insisted that God, and no other was the creator. He created not from the corpses of malevolent enemy gods, but simply and solely by his Word. He spoke words of creation, active, effective, powerful, "God said, let there be light, and there was light. God saw how good the light was."

Continuing through the six days of creation, the authors use the seventh to remind the Jews why they have almost ceased to be the covenant community, why their faith is so weak. After creation God rested on the sabboath. If the Jews had had enough sense to do the same, turning toward God and listening to his Word, they would not find themselves in their present despair.

However, the story of creation was intended not so much to tell the exiles what he had done in the past, as what his creative Word could still do in the present. A contemporary prophet in Isaiah 40,41 proclaims the same message: from the present chaos God's Word can bring about a new creation.

Neither the priests of Genesis I nor the prophet of Isaiah 40,41 drew this message out of thin air. It was the result of prayerful meditation on their experience. The passover itself had been a result of his creative Word, forming them into the new creation of covenant community from the chaos of slavery in

Egypt. That Word of creation, power and invitation was still being spoken.

At Sinai they had been told that response to that Word was the very condition that would prevent their returning to chaos. "If you hearken to my voice" (Ex 19:5) was no idle formula. They could ignore the Word, take it for granted, pietistically enclose it in phylacteries or abandon it to liturgical formalism, but only at the risk of ceasing to be covenant community. It was only by listening to it, that they would know their own charism, their own identity.

Before the exile Amos had warned them:

Yes, days are coming, says the Lord God, when I will send famine upon the land: Not a famine of bread, or thirst for water, but for hearing the word of the Lord. Then shall they wander from sea to sea and rove from the north to the east in search of the word of the Lord, but they shall not find it (Am 8:11,12).

But the exile was no time for recrimination, but rather for hope and encouragement.

For my thoughts are not your thoughts, nor are your ways my ways, says the Lord. As high as the heavens are above the earth; so high are my ways above your ways and my thoughts above your thoughts. For just as from the heavens the rain and snow come down and do not return there till they have watered the earth, making it fertile and fruitful, giving seed to him who sows and bread to him who eats, so shall my word be that goes forth from my mouth; it shall not return to me void, but shall do my will, achieving the end for which I sent it. Yes, in joy you shall depart, in peace you shall be brought back. (Is 55:8–12).

He is not man who bables words, but God, whose

Word creates. His Word is as certain and creative as the very cycles of the creation which he brought into existence.

Little is known of the confused histroy after the return from exile in 537. But the editing of the Bible and the emergence of the synagogue connote a renewed enthusiasm for the Word. However, it was only a comparatively short time until the prophetic word, if it was sent, was not received. Inspired writers had to attribute their work to ancient figures such as Job, Daniel and Jonah to get a hearing. Divine communication not written in Hebrew was practically ignored.

It was as if the decision had been made that in the words they had God had spoken all he had to say. But his ways are not our ways.

In times past, God spoke in fragmentary and varied ways to our fathers through the prophets; in this, the final age, he has spoken to us through his Son, whom he has made heir of all things and through whom he first created the universe (Heb 1:1,2).

The fragmentary and varied ways were fulfilled in one Word: "The Word became flesh and made his dwelling among us" (Jn 1:14). Yet his own, to whom he had never grown weary of speaking his word, did not accept him.

In his prologue, John in conscious imitation of the first words of creation in Genesis shows that Jesus Christ is *the* Word of God with the same function as the Word in creation. He brings about the new creation, the community of God's people. In the power of that Word men could become what they had failed to be by their own efforts, the covenant community of the people of God. "Any who did accept him, he empowered to become God's children."

Like creation, it is a continuing, growing process, not accomplished once, and then over and done with. "He empowered to become." It continues through the power of his Word. "The words I spoke to you are spirit and life," he announced at the end of the Eucharistic discourse. In the same scene Peter shows a recognition of the source of his growth as disciple and leader of the community. "Lord, to whom shall we go? You have the words of eternal life" (Jn 6:63,68).

Even to a woman who had praised his mother for her physical relationship to him, Jesus replied that the blessedness of any person does not arise from flesh or blood but response to the Word. "A woman from the crowd called out, 'Blest is the womb that bore you and the breasts that nursed you!' 'Rather,' he replied, 'blest are they who hear the word of God and keep it'" (Lk 11:27,28), and "My mother and my brothers are those who hear the word of God and act upon it" (Lk 8:21).

Community, which is nothing less than the Body of Christ, is not formed any differently from when the Body of Christ was first formed: "Be it done unto me according to your *word*." God has not changed his plan. Among the many voices that speak of community, there is but one that can accomplish it. There can be no community that does not consist of hearers of the Word, enthusiastically sharing it with each other. If communities are tempted to give more priority to meals than to the Word, then from the midst of his own temptation Jesus says again: "Not on bread alone does man live, but by every word that comes from the mouth of God" (Mt 4:4).

5.

———————COMMUNITY OF FAITH

According to the letter of the Pontifical Biblical Commission to Cardinal Suhard in 1948, the first eleven chapters of Genesis are not to be labeled history in the modern sense of the term. While the Biblical Commission does not identify their literary form, most Biblical scholars today would label them "myth."

Too many people are frightened off by such terminology, because they equate it with their childhood idea of fairy tale rather than the technical meaning that theologians and Scripture scholars give it today. Myth, in this sense, is not a fable or an untrue yarn. It is a term used to describe a literary form which very often contains more truth than an historical account does. It encompasses truth, not just about a past event, but about you and me in the present. It is man's effort to clothe the deepest realities about God and himself in human words, that are always inadequate for such a task. Myth is man's feeble attempt to express the inexpressible.

The eleventh chapter of Genesis, the story of the tower of Babel or Babylon, is myth in this sense. It portrays that deep and universal longing in man to make something of himself and form community.

Come, let us build ourselves a city and a tower with its top in the sky, and so make a name for ourselves; otherwise we shall be scattered all over the earth.

Yet, the very unity they sought to achieve by their own efforts is shattered by the resultant inability even to communicate with each other in the same language. The author is not just trying to tell us about a past event (indeed there were great towers in Babylon). He is telling us about ourselves, and our futile efforts• to build community and communicate among ourselves.

But he does not leave us hanging. He leaps from the myth which speaks of all of us, to the stage of history where we find Abraham, our father in faith (Genesis 12). At the tower they babbled, but Abraham, speaking not one word, says "yes " to God with his life. Then, God speaks, and community results. "I will make of you a great nation, and I will bless you; I will make your name great so that you will be a blessing" (Gn 12.2). These are the very things that the strenuous efforts at Babel tried to bring about.

The author's iuxtaposition of these chapters is intentional. Works won't do it. Faith will. After all the breakdown of community that resulted from sin, Abraham emerges as the man of faith in whom are all hopes for community. He does not try to make something of himself, make a name for himself, but in silence, simply stands open to God. From that day to this, his faith stands as the model for all who live in faith, striving after community.

The Hebrew word for faith has the same root as the affirmation with which we conclude every prayer:

Amen.

When a Hebrew spoke of faith, he knew that it meant to be firm, to be well grounded. It has the connotation of having a trustworthy anchor so as not to be buffeted or tossed about. For Abraham faith was not to recite a creed, but to say yes to a person without whom life would be precarious and fragile.

He expresses his faith by putting all his trust and hope in God, even when, humanly speaking, God's promises, and his own yearnings seem impossible of fulfillment. Promised that he would be a great nation, his wife remains sterile, and when she finally gives birth, Abraham is ordered to sacrifice his son! Yet Abraham never wavers, because he knows that faith implies that someone beyond himself is running the show.

He is our father in faith, but before he comes to that faith, there are certain presuppositions. He must let go of all that made him feel secure before. "Go forth from the land of your kinsfolk and your father's house" (Gn 12:1). Abraham is offered life with God, but only if he will relinquish the human security that his arms reached out for and be willing to be grasped in the arms of the living God.

From a people who claimed Abraham as their father, but who had become preoccupied with a self-satisfying legalism and the self-complacency of being "chosen," Jesus demanded faith in himself. "If you were Abraham's children, you would be following Abraham's example. . .Why do you not believe me?" (Jn 8:39 ff.) Because they were so tenacious of their own security, and so often confused their own aspirations and goals with God's call, they were not able to respond.

But, of those who did respond Jesus demanded the same faith as his father demanded of Abraham. Occupation and family are what give a person a sense of identity. Yet, of the disciples Matthew tells us: "He called them and immediately they abandoned boat and father to follow him" (Mt 4:22).

St. Paul, with his struggle in the primitive Christian community with those who wanted to compromise faith by insisting on joining it to obedience to laws and regulations (cf. Philippians 3, Galatians and Romans), is the man who learned the hard way what faith really is. It is important to remember that his conversion is not from sin or conscious alienation from God. When we celebrate his conversion, we celebrate the turning from efforts to save himself by obedience to the law, toward the person of Jesus Christ.

As a Jew he had considered himself a man of great "faith." He was a Jew of strict observance, priding himself on adhering to the "holier than thou" sect of the pharisees. He felt that his adherence to the minute demands of the law brought him very close to God. For him religion was faith in the power of the law to save him.

In legal observance I was a Pharisee, and so zealous that I persecuted the church. I was above reproach when it came to justice based on the law. But those things I used to consider gain I have now reappraised as loss in the light of Christ. I have come to rate all as loss in the light of the surpassing knowledge of my Lord Jesus Christ. For his sake I have forfeited everything; I have accounted all else rubbish so that

Christ may be my wealth and I may be in him, not having any justice of my own based on observance of the law. The justice I possess is that which comes through faith in Christ. It has its origin in God and is based on faith. I wish to know Christ and the power flowing from his resurrection (Phil 3:5b–10a).

He had come to realize that faith is not a set of observances, but life with a person. His conversion was in letting go of those things which he thought had made him holy. From a life dominated by religious observance, he turned to a life dominated by the Lord.

And even though this conversion is depicted as a sudden event in Acts, Paul lets us know that it is an ongoing process, that takes place in community. Following his conversion (Acts 9) he went to the community for strength and growth in faith. He knew his faith had to grow. "I am racing to grasp the prize, if possible, since I have been grasped by Christ Jesus (Phil 3:12).

We, like Paul, have a fragile faith, but like him, we come to community to have it strengthened. We come not to a community that has arrived, but who are struggling believers, pilgrims. There is a bit of Babel in each of us. We try to do God's work and form the perfect community. But it will come in no other way than it did to Abraham and Paul, standing together in openness to God.

6.

LIFE WITH THE LORD
—DISCIPLESHIP

The religion from which Paul converted was a religion that in many ways no longer preserved Abraham's vision of faith. It was to this vision that Paul returned.

Hence, all depends on faith, everything is grace. Thus the promise holds true for all Abraham's descendants, not only for those who have the law but for all who have his faith. He is father of us all. For our faith will be credited to us also if we believe in him who raised Jesus our Lord from the dead (Rom 4:16,24).

Certainly what happened among the Jews was not a conscious subversion of faith. It was a process that culminated in the post-exilic period (537 on) as a very praiseworthy attempt to preserve their identity as God's people. In danger of being absorbed first by the Babylonians, and later by the Persians, Greeks and Romans, they could well have gone the way of many other peoples who disappeared in history. The books of Maccabees show how very real that possibility was.

Strict adherence to all the newly-codified laws of the past helped them retain a sense of identity. They could be conscious that they were different by their feasts, celebrations, food, customs and ritual. The good Jew was the one who observed them all meticulously.

But since such prescriptions ran into the hundreds, the best Jew was the one who knew and observed the law best. Ezra had gone so far as to identify the multitudinous ordinances of the law as that "from which men draw life, when they practice them" (Neh 9:29).

What had begun as a noble effort to preserve identity eventually evolved into a confusion of law with religion. Lawyers and rabbis become the religious leaders, attracting to themselves disciples whose lives were devoted to discussing the fine points of the law and its interpretation.

Paul had prided himself on being a disciple of Gamaliel, one of the greatest legal experts of Judaism (Acts 22:3). Such would be the cherished boast of any Jew who was trying to be religious, to have sat at the feet of a great rabbi as his disciple.

There is, however, probably no. more clear distinction between the religion of Jesus and that of the rabbis than in their concept of discipleship. The Gospels witness that Jesus was frequently called rabbi, and his followers, disciples, but it was a similarity in name only.

There was a difference in the call. Pious Jews sought out famed rabbis to sit at their feet. With his disciples the initiative is on the part of Jesus. "It was not you who chose me, it was I who chose you" (Jn 15:16).

The rabbis would accept only the most promising candidates, those with the highest I.Q. and cleverness in disputation. They were very interested in the quality of the men who would hand on their own name and teachings. Jesus, however, seems to have gone out of his way to choose the most unlikely, unsuited candidates, with nothing to offer. Paul sums up the situation well:

Brothers, you are among those called. Consider your situation. Not many of you are wise, as men account wisdom; not many are influential; and surely not many are well-born. God chose those whom the world considers absurd to shame the wise; he singled out the weak of this world to shame the strong. He chose the world's lowborn and despied, those who count for nothing, to reduce to nothing those who were something; so that mankind can do no boasting before God. God it is who has given you life in Christ Jesus (I Cor 1:26–30a).

Jesus chooses the most ill-suited candidates, so that they would never forget the source of their power. "He who lives in me and I in him will produce fruit abundantly, for apart from me you can do nothing" (Jn 15:5).

The story of Martha and Mary, far from being a lesson in the contemplative life is a lesson in the revolution Jesus was effecting. Mary's better part is that she has put aside all that Martha is preoccupied with and taken the place of a disciple at the Master's feet. No self-respecting rabbi in that male-dominated religion would have tolerated it. Jesus opens discipleship to all.

Since the rabbis were interested in seeing that their opinions and decisions were handed on intact, the disciples of Jesus would not even have passed the entrance exam. If they had thought that memorizing the words of Jesus was a goal, they failed miserably. The Gospels manifest variations in such important words of Jesus as the Our Father, and the formula of the consecration of the bread and wine at the last supper.

They knew that they had not come to Jesus to memorize his words, much less to dispute with him. His words were important only because they were an invitation to life with him. If they had come to him for his teaching, the disciples on the road to Emmaus should not have been so grief-stricken. They still had his teaching. Their attitude shows that they had come to him not so much for a way of life, but for life, and they feared it was lost.

This same attitude is manifested in the amount of control Jesus demanded over the lives of his disciples. The Jewish rabbis tried only to affect the thinking of their disciples concerning the law. Jesus takes possession of every aspect of the lives of his disciples. With semitic hyperbole that leaves no doubt of his demands upon his disciples, he will not permit priority to be given to burial of parents over life with himself (Mt 8:21).

Life totally with Jesus: that is discipleship; and nothing less will do. He controls the prayer of the disciples, their apostolate and how they are to conduct themselves. His disciples recognized his all embracing and radical demands. They knew they were not like other disciples who would graduate from the care of the rabbi whose teaching they followed, and then go out and get disciples for themselves.

Their role was to go out and make disciples for Jesus, not for themselves.

Full authority has been given to me both in heaven and on

earth; go, therefore, and make disciples of all the nations. Baptize them in the name of the Father, and of the Son, and of the Holy Spirit. Teach them to carry out everything I have commanded you. And know that I am with you always, until the end of the world (Mt 28:18b–20)!

He is not a rabbi who has simply bequeathed to them his teaching. He is with them, and that constitutes their discipleship.

Some of them later wrote Gospels but not to satisfy the curiosity and interest of a generation that had not walked with Jesus. They wrote to invite that generation. They wrote to call them to live with Jesus. They, too, could become disciples, and walk with him even now, for he was with them to the end of the world.

Yet each of the Gospels portrays a different picture of Jesus. Each one of them manifests a grasp of Jesus as perceived by different disciples and communities of disciples. He is not stereotyped, but emerges with a richness which is only possible because the early Church cherished different points of view.

The very existence of four Gospels rather than one, of four different ways of proclaiming him who calls, highlights the role of each disciple.

Each must live with Jesus so intimately and express him in his life so clearly, that he, too, is writing a Gospel. As Matthew's differs from John's so mine may differ from yours, but both will proclaim an invitation to life with him.

Jewish community was centered on exact observance of law. The community of Christians is united by the reality of Jesus Christ, not by rule or even by apostolate. Both may flow from discipleship, but foremost we are disciples of Jesus Christ, and he's not a rabbi who joins people together by a common viewpoint on laws and regulations.

7.

_____IT IS THE LORD WHO CALLS

One of the most puzzling things of New Testament times is that short but tragic phrase of John's prologue, "To his own he came, yet his own did not accept him." Why, when we see Christianity so widespread today, was Jesus accepted by so few in his own lifetime?

It is obvious that Jesus' call demanded a conversion that not many were willing to make. What were the attitudes that paralyzed them, making them unwilling to take that step toward him?

The situation, which was already puzzling to the second generation of Christians who wrote the Gospels, is complicated and cannot be resolved by oversimplification calling it bad will.

There were many attitudes in Judaism that emerged to solidify the resistance to Jesus. One was his attitude toward the law. For the pious Jew the law was a gift of God. In Psalm 119 his ancestors had sung of it, praising it or a synonym for it in every one of its one hundred and seventy-six lines. Verse 98 is a good summary of the pious Jew's attitude: "Your command has made me wiser than my enemies, for it is ever with me." The boast of the Jew was that he did not have to second-guess God. He knew his will and what was demanded of him by the Lord. This made him different from the pagans, the playthings of their gods, who never knew what the gods were up to, or what they wanted of men. For the Jew the law was religion and religion was the law.

Jesus' attitude toward the law did not exactly endear him to them. While he spoke of the necessity of its fulfillment (Mt 5:17 ff.), he had no kind words for its exponents. Because of what he said (Mt 15), "Pharisee," once a term of honor, has become a synonym for hypocrite. There is no doubt that his attitude, that he was superior to the law, was a major cause of the enmity of the leaders of Judaism. Their encounters with him most frequently center on the breaking of the sabbath, of which he claimed to be Lord (e.g. Mk 2:23).

But the problem, not just with the authorities, but with many of the common people as well, lay not with his attitude toward the law, but theirs. For them religion, life in covenant, was a way of living. It was a detailed plan of activity for living well and godly. It was a well organized carrying out of religious activity, covering every contingency of life. The law was the unerring guide. In it they found the way and the truth that would assure them of the good life. They had so long confused religion with adherence to a plan of living that they could not believe (Jn 12:39) that it was adherence to a person. "I am the way, the truth and the life" (Jn 14:6) was too much for them.

Another attitude that militated against his acceptance was their own expectation. They had hopes for a messiah who would solve all of their problems. The difficulty was that they envisioned their problems as being external. It could be summed up in their domination by Rome. If they were to be God's people then they must have their own nation and become their own masters. This was the very attitude that encouraged the Zealots in their guerrilla activities and eventually brought down the wrath of Rome upon them. The nation, city, and temple were devastated in 70 A.D.

It was for this reason that Jesus was reluctant to accept the term "messiah." When he does accept it from the lips of Peter (Mk 8:27; Mt 16:13) it is on his terms, not Peter's. He will be a suffering servant, not a warrior. This hardly fit the pattern of what the vast majority of Jews had decided the messiah should be and do. He just didn't live up to their expectations.

Another, and perhaps the most important factor that militated against the acceptance of him as fulfilling the hopes of Israel was that he was just too human. The very name that God had revealed to Moses in the burning bush (Ex 3), Yahweh, should have let them know that he was with them, close to them. But the hyper-literal interpretation of the law had eventually led them to interpret the second commandment as not speaking his name at all. Eventually it was known only to the high priest and spoken only in the silence of the Holy of Holies once a year. The God who had revealed himself as near was kept at a distance.

He had revealed himself to have the tender human love of a husband and parent (Hosea 2,11), but because religion was perceived as law, he came to be perceived as the distant and fierce judge. The awe at the transcendence of God was necessary, of course, to counter the temptation to be like the pagans who manipulated their gods. But this brought an over re-action, keeping at a distance the God who desired to be close. Such an attitude left no room for ac-ceptance of the all too human Jesus. This was no way for the God of the marvels of the Exodus, and the magnificent glory of Sinai to reveal himself.

Mark's picture of him as needing time for prayer (1:35), being angry at their lack of openness (3:5), being thought of as insane by his own relatives (3:21), and being impatient with the dullness of his own disciples (4:13; 7:18) made him appear all too much like themselves. How can one who angrily drives peo-ple out of a house, just because they laughed at him (5:40), be anything more than the carpenter, and one of themselves (6:3)? "They found him too much for them" is an understatement. For all the authority with which he preached and the signs he performed, his humanity was *the* stumbling block, the scandal.

And it did not cease to be a major obstacle to be-lief even after his Resurrection. He was too much for many in the early Church who also had their own ideas as to how God should reveal himself. They ad-hered to one of the earliest heresies to emerge, Doce-tism. From the Greek Word meaning "to seem, to ap-pear," it maintained that since there is something wrong with flesh and matter, it is blasphemy to say that God was made man. He only appeared so; it was a phantom. To these people, so disdainful of the material world and their own flesh we owe many of the apocryphal stories about Jesus. They make his divinity an escape valve for the pressures of his humanity. He makes clay sparrows, and sends them flying. He solves the problems of juvenile delinquency by telling a couple of teenagers to drop dead and they do. For them a Jesus with dirty feet and human needs was impossible.

Against them John proclaims the Word made flesh. "What we have seen with out eyes, what we have looked upon and our hands have touched—we speak of the word of life" (1 Jn 1:1b).

Paul insists that he did not have some ideal humanity, unlike our own: "God sent his son in the likeness of sinful flesh" (Rom 8:3). He knows our humanity, its struggles and temptations, for he "had a full share in ours" (Heb 2:14; cf. 4:15).

The Jews would have accepted him as military leader or wonder worker. He refused to be accepted on any other terms but his own, even by Peter (Mt. 16:22,23).

He it is who calls us, who forms us into community. But we must accept him for what he is, not what we expect him to be. Perhaps our art has not helped us, with its velvet clad babies or Hollywood—handsome figures walking on clouds. But religious above all should have a clear vision of Jesus' humanity. Otherwise they will not be able to appreciate their own, and that is a major obstacle to discipleship and community. We are disciples of a real person who gives not so much a plan of life, but himself.

8.

LOVING ONE ANOTHER
_____AS HE LOVED US

When a husband calls his wife honey or sweetheart, he is hardly referring to her calorie content. Language always limps when we try to describe deep relationships, and so we must use analogies.

The Biblical authors faced the same problem: how to verbalize mysteries so deep and relationships so incredible that they defied human expression. They had to take instances of their own experience and say "our life with God and each other is *like* that." And in the very description they knew that they had fallen short of capturing such a reality in a few words.

The relationship of covenant community was first conceived by the Israelites as being like a treaty in which the participants were bound together by steadfast loyalty or *hesed*. This word grew in its connotation so that instead of just referring to a political relationship it began to refer to the enduring love of a personal relationship. This was much more expressive of the bond between Yahweh and his people who were called not to be just a political entity, but a kingdom of priests and a holy nation.

It is this meaning of *hesed* that the 8th century prophet Hosea used when he condemned Israel for its absence among them (Hos 4:1 ff.). That he equates it both with a lack of "knowledge of God in the land,"

and with their crimes against each other shows that this love is to be the binding force of their life with Yahweh and in community with each other.

"Knowledge," here as elsewhere in the Bible, must be understood in the semitic sense. Speculative knowledge or even knowledge *about* someone or something was alien to the semitic mentality. For the Israelite, knowledge was always practical and referred to life and experience. That is why he used the same word to describe the life-sharing experience of a man and woman. "Adam knew his wife Eve, and she bore a son." The two became one, however, not just in a sexual encounter, but in lives united and shared. This was real knowing. Thus, the Israelites' lack of knowledge of God was not a lack of familiarity with facts about him, catechism knowledge. They were not living with him, in his presence and love. They did not know him, even if they knew about him.

Hosea arrives at his condemnation of his people for their lack of love (*hesed*) and knowledge in a startling way: the tragic experience of his personal married life (Hos 1–3). His own ill-fated marriage to a nymphomaniac becomes the analogue for Israel's relationship with her husband, Yahweh. The underlying message of the prophet is: if you really want to know what life in a covenant community should be like, look at an ideal marriage. The tender, selfless, enduring love of husband and wife will show you what your life with God and each other should be like.

He, of course, depicts the opposite: a marriage gone sour, due to growing lukewarmness, selfishness, lack of concern and consideration and forgetfulness. Yet the outward pretense, the external structures and signs are still observed. Such is pure hypocrisy when there is no *hesed*.

In depicting their unconcern for true covenant, Hosea uses another word for love. He names one of his children Lo-Ruhama, Unloved. This comes from the word *raham*, womb, and was meant to express the tender love of a mother for her children and of the offspring of the same womb for each other.

Hosea's yearning for Yahweh's steadfast and tender love to be reciprocated finds its echo in the scene of Jesus weeping over Jerusalem whose people would not return his love (Lk 19:41 ff.). He had already told them (Mt 22:39,40; cp. Lk 10:27 ff.) that no law or even the utterance of a prophet (hence the whole of the Old Testament) had any meaning unless it depended upon the love of God and neighbor. Nothing makes sense without love. He cut through their legalism and formalism to pose just one question about any structure of religion, "What does it have to do with love?"

And even this teaching in the Synoptic Gospels is surpassed by John's meditation on Jesus. Loving others as ourselves becomes:

I give you a new commandment: Love one another. Such as my love has been for you, so must your love be for each other. This is how all will know you for my disciples: your love for one another (Jn 13:34,35).

Surrounded by men who thought that spiritual life was identified with legal observance and who.wore

external signs to show their great piety, Jesus offered
his disciples no other credential for discipleship than
their love for one another. It is to be the same love
as he shares with the Father (Jn 15:9)—a selfless,
giving love. "Of his fullness we have all had a share—
love following upon love. For while the law came
through Moses, this enduring love came through Jesus
Christ" (Jn 1:15,16).

This is my commandment: love one another as I have loved
you. There is no greater love than this: to lay down one's life
for one's friends (Jn 15:12-13).

Even before this, Paul realized that the laying down
of one's life is not a unique, solitary act. It is not
just what Jesus did on Good Friday, but every day
of his life. It is the giving, sharing, strengthening
love that Jesus always manifested. Paul describes this,
the only love worthy to be called Christian in his first
letter to the Corinthians.

They thought they were bound together by being a
fan club for one or another personality (1:12) or by
their sharing a kind of superior knowledge and spirituality (2:6). After telling them how really intimately
they are united as a community (You, then, are the
Body of Christ: 12:27) he tells them how to show
forth this bond of community (I Cor 13).

A community that is really Christian is marked by
patience and kindness, not by jealousy, airs or snob-
ishness. Rudeness, self-seeking, anger and brooding
over injuries have no part in it. Members of such a
community never put limits on forbearance, trust,
hope or love's power to endure. And no matter what

activity or apostolate that community involves itself in, without love, they are as useful as the noise made by a gong.

Among the several words for love available to him in Greek, Paul chose one, *agape*. It has the meaning of a selfless, unmerited love. It is really love of the unlovable. It never asks if the object of the love is worth it.

Such love is impossible for us, and we would not even have known of it, had we not first experienced it.

God's love was revealed in our midst in this way: he sent his only Son to the world that we might have life through him. Love, then, consists in this: not that we have loved God, but that he has loved us and has sent his Son as an offering for our sins. Beloved, if God has loved us so, we must have the same love for one another (I Jn 4:9-11).

It is only possible because he lives in us. Christian community is nothing without it. Any apostolate, goal or rule that claims to bring people together is simply a counterfeit of Christian community without it. It may be difficult, but religious above all should be the ones to show that it is not a pipe dream or a chimera. The life of any religious community is nothing if it is not a voice that shouts: "We can love, for he first loved us."

9.

_____COMMUNITY OF PRAYER

Since prayer is a communication between persons in love, the quality of prayer in a community is a good barometer of the state of the relationship. Biblical prayer flourishes at times when the individual and community are most aware of the presence of God as a person in their midst, and deeply conscious of his gift of love. They find that the response of faith, saying "yes" to him with their lives, is but the beginning of a relationship in which there can be no silent partners. He does not need me, but he constantly calls.

He has no need to hear me, but he constantly listens. Prayer only makes sense in light of that fact: my awareness of a God who listens and cares. Then, I must pray. For if I have experienced what life is like with him then I am also aware of what it would be like without him. Prayer then becomes the necessary expression of a life lived in covenant.

Covenant life is a prayer in itself. But if such a statement implies that activity, even for God, can take the place of prayer, then it might be well to meditate once again on Hosea's analogy of marriage and covenant life with the Lord. The marriage which finds the partners in constant activity for each other with no time for communication with each other will

soon be marriage in name only. As the "I do" of the
ceremony is but the beginning of words spoken to
express the relationship, so is the "yes" of the covenant.

To presume that the call once given, and the response once made are over and done with, is to find
oneself in the company of so many in the Old Testament who rejoiced in being chosen, and then went
their own merry way. In I Cor 10:7 Paul quotes Exodus 33:6, seeing here the very reason for the bank-
ruptcy of the people of the covenant. "They sat down
to eat and drink (i.e. covenant meal) and arose to
take their pleasure." They did not pray, because just
that quickly they had forgotten how much they needed
God.

It is a Biblical axiom that if the forgetful man does
not pray, neither does the proud man. At best, conscious of his own activity, he informs God how good
he has been. The implication is, that if God has any
sense, he will continue to be good to him, since he
has been good to God. Jesus gives the prayer of the
Pharisee as the prime example of this attitude (Lk
18:9). His words were addressed to God, but that did
not make it prayer. It was simply the settling of ac-
counts. By giving the pleas of the tax collector as
the example of authentic prayer Jesus cuts through
the formalism of his time. The Publican admits that
he has been a sinner.

The Biblical concept of sin is "to miss the mark,
miss the goal." He has sinned because he has gone
after every goal but God. He has gone his own way,
done his own thing. His prayer expresses that he has

found that goal, and so he cries for mercy—not pity, but *heses,* the covenant relationship that only God can give. The Pharisee was aware of God as the divine wholesaler, so he negotiated. The Publican was aware of the God who calls to a love that he could never achieve by himself, and so he prayed. It was the professional religious, the Pharisee, who missed the mark.

The Publican is a New Testament representative of that poor, prophetic group of the old. They were constantly seeking the will of the Lord, while their leaders "rose to take their pleasure." They took God seriously. They were the prayers of the psalms whose hunger and thirst for God was more real than their bodily needs.

As the hind longs for the running waters, so my soul longs for you, O God. Athirst is my soul for God, the living God. When shall I go and behold the face of God (Ps 42:2,3)?

A contemporary of Jeremiah, Zephaniah, over six hundred years before Christ describes these people of the Psalms.

For then will I remove from your midst the proud braggarts, and you shall no longer exalt yourself on my holy mountain. But I will leave as a remnant in your midst a people humble and lowly, who shall take refuge in the name of the Lord: the remnant of Israel (Zep 3:11,12).

Authentic prayer, calling upon the name of the Lord, is the role of the remnant, the community within the community, the poor ones of the Lord.

At the same time, Jeremiah whose life well represented the aspirations of the remnant is also the authentic man of prayer. He prays, not in formulae, but in words that confess his own confusion and weakness, and he even tells God off, when he thought God was a bit confused and was falling down on the job (Jer 20:7 ff.)!

His prayer includes cursing and pleas for vengeance as do the Psalms. If this is an affront to our gentility or "Christian charity" it may not be just because we do not express ourselves in a semitic mentality. It may be because we lack their enthusiasm for God and his covenant and growth in it that literally screamed out for removal of obstacles to it. Perhaps we are unwilling to perceive our self-complacency, self-righteousness, lack of trust, polarization or even indifference to prayer itself as the children whose heads must be dashed upon a stone.

Biblical prayer such as this is the result of an intense familiarity with God. He is more real to them than any person in their experience. He is not a god enthroned afar gazing in majestic indifference, like the pagan gods whose interest must be stirred by a constant repetition of formulae. "In your prayer, do not rattle on like the pagans. They think they will win a hearing by the sheer multiplication of words" (Mt 6:7).

In this same sermon, Jesus taught his disciples to pray. In him the love of God was made manifest and they were in a relationship with God deeper than had ever been possible. God was more real to them than he had ever been. What could they say?

"This is how you are to pray: Our Father" (Mt

6:9 ff.). Luke's variant version (11:2) shows that Jesus was not teaching another formula, but a spirit of prayer: how to pray. No one before had experienced the intimacy that would enable him to call God, Father. Paul grasped this intimacy when he retained the Aramaic *Abba* (Daddy) in Romans 8:15, a name that can again be heard today on the streets of Jerusalem from a child calling out to his daddy. He speaks to him as the most real person in his life, as the source of it, from whom he has learned to love. Jesus says we can do the same.

It sounds easy, but even Paul knew that prayer could be difficult. But it is not impossible, for the Spirit is with us, if we will be quiet and let him speak.

The Spirit too helps us in our weakness, for we do not know how to pray as we ought; but the Spirit himself makes intercession for us with groanings that cannot be expressed in speech (Rom 8:26).

And the more we pray, the more will he be there, for Luke (11:13) in a delightful development of the words of the Lord (cp. Mt 7:11) based upon his own experience of prayer, tells us that the Holy Spirit himself is the answer to every prayer.

The people of the covenant, both old and new, never *asked* if they *had* to pray together; they were amazed that they could. And if they had not, none of the prayers of the Bible would ever be known to us. We have the Psalms, the Magnificat and the Our Father itself, because individuals shared their prayer and the community made them their own. Luke tells us (24:53) that after the Ascension the Christian community turned immediately to praying together. They knew that the community of the Resurrection is nothing if it is not a community of prayer.

Christ's peace must reign in your hearts, since as members of the one body you have been called to that peace. Dedicate yourselves to thankfulness. Let the word of Christ, rich as it is, dwell in you. In wusdom made perfect, instruct and admonish one another. Sing gratefully to God from your hearts in psalms, hymns, and inspired songs.

If we find a different message in the signs of the times, then we have misread them.

10.

PEOPLE IN LOVE
_____MAKE SIGNS OF LOVE

The title of this chapter is taken from a document of the American Bishops on Music in the Liturgy published several years ago. It is a happy phrase that is an excellent definition of liturgy. People in love make signs of love, in order to express their love, and at the same time deepen it. The faith community is a people in love, and if they do not express their relationship in sign, it will die. As married love will weaken and disintegrate when not expressed in sign, so will covenant love.

At Sinai, immediately after the people ratified the covenant, saying "We will do everything that the Lord has told us" (Ex 24:3), Moses showed them how to celebrate their new relationship in sign.

The first sign is that of sacrifice. Primitive as they were, the Israelites did not think that they had a God who loved blood and dead animals. God did not need dead animals any more than he needed the Israelites. He didn't need the sacrifice; they did. They had to express their faith and love and remind themselves of their new relationship in covenant.

In covenant they gave the best thing they had, themselves, to God. They signified this in sacrifice by giving the next-to-the best thing they had, animals from their flock. The gift of the animal spoke of the

55

gift of themselves. The blood poured out, which for them was life itself, spoke of a life poured out in union with God. The sprinkling of life-blood upon altar and people spoke of lives united in covenant. "Then he took the blood and sprinkled it on the people, saying, 'This is the blood of the covenant which the Lord has made with you in accordance with all these words of his'" (Ex 24:8). The death of the animal signified a new state of existence, consumed totally in God, as the people of the covenant were to be.

The sacrifice completed, Moses then gives them another sign of their covenant love (Ex 24:12). With representatives of the people he shares a covenant meal. Such a sharing of food always bespeaks a sharing of lives. The very word, "companion" comes from the latin *"cum pane,"* with bread. With families, the sharing of food and drink says something about relationship. As they share, it also becomes a time for them to talk and sing about the "good old days." They reminisce about those things that have made them to be what they are. Much of the early portions of the Bible, including the entire story of the exodus, and many of the psalms, originated in such a setting.

Sacrifice and meal, both were actions and signs which spoke of a relationship lived out in daily life. The Israelite liturgy differed radically from the pagan. The Israelites worshiped to show that their lives were in the control of God. The pagans worshiped in order to control the gods.

When the people began to think that if God were happy with one dead lamb he would be delighted with ten, they began to confuse the quantity of sacrifice with the quality of their covenant lives, which sacrifice signified. When sacrifice was used to manipulate God rather than be a sign of a life in his love, then they were no better off than the pagans. Worship is a sign of love or it is hypocrisy.

Worship, a means to express covenant, became an end in itself. The prophets, so ready to distinguish means from ends, and appearances from reality, could not tolerate the dichotomy between life and its signs.

Amos, with a directness that might not be a bad thing to hear in our pulpits today, expresses the attitude of all the prophets.

Hear this word, women of the mountain of Samaria, you cows of Bashan, you who oppress the weak and abuse the needy; who say to your lords, "Bring drink for us!" The Lord God has sworn by his holiness: Truly the days are coming upon you when they shall drag you away with hooks, the last of you with fishhooks; you shall go out through the breached walls each by the most direct way, and you shall be cast into the mire, says the Lord. Come to Bethel and sin, to Gilgal, and sin the more; each morning bring your sacrifices, every third day, your tithes; burn leavened food as a thanksgiving sacrifice, proclaim publicly your freewill offerings, for so you love to do, O men of Israel, says the Lord God (Am 4:1-5).

They would be better off not coming to church, where they sinned more, by adding hypocrisy to their infidelity.

The exile, with no liturgy, was meant to help them get covenant back in focus. But even then they thought that Yahweh would be just a bit happier with blood, smoke and incense than with their lives in covenant.

We have in our day no prince, prophet, or leader, no holo-
caust, sacrifice, oblation, or incense, no place to offer first fruits,
to find favor with you. But with contrite heart and humble
spirit let us be received; as though it were holocausts of rams
and bullocks, or thousands of fat lambs, so let our sacrifice
be in your presence today as we follow you unreservedly; for
those who trust in you cannot be put to shame (Dn 3:38-40).

They still could not quite believe that God would
be happier with live people in covenant rather than
with dead animals in sacrifice.

When they did return from exile and rebuilt the
temple it was with a narrow vision of covenant. Pure
Jewish blood became the criterion for covenant mem-
bership, and so they would not even let the Samari-
tans participate in the rebuilding of the temple (Neh
4:1-3).

Later on it was to a Samaritan that Jesus, who had
just revealed himself as *the* Temple of God (Jn 2:21),
made known the attitude that he required in liturgy.

An hour is coming, and is already here, when authentic worshipers will worship the Father in Spirit and truth. Indeed,
it is just such worshipers the Father seeks. God is Spirit, and
those who worship him must worship in Spirit and truth (Jn
4:23,24).

God is not satisfied with external forms or rituals.
They must be real signs, speaking of what is in the
heart.

Jesus himself gave such a sign on the night before
he died. He took the elements of the passover meal,
which already spoke of liberation from slavery and

freedom to enter covenant. Quoting Moses at Sinai, he gave a new meaning to the signs. "This is my blood, the blood of the covenant to be poured out on behalf of many" (Mk 14:24).

What a marvelous experience to have been there. How could anyone miss the point of what was happening? How could anyone be less than a worshiper in spirit and in truth? According to Luke, the wonder lasted about two minutes!! Jesus put the cup down, and spoke of his betrayal, while the disciples argued about first place.

True, never again could the signs become empty or hypocritical, for they were the Body and Blood of Jesus Christ. But they could fail to have their effect on those who did not know what covenant is all about.

Paul knew what Eucharist effected. "We, though many, are one body, because we all partake of the same bread" (I Cor 10:17). The Eucharistic Body on the altar brings a unity which effects the bond of covenant to such an extent that Christians can now be called the Body of Christ. But that will be a reality only for those who have some comprehension of what covenant community is all about, and have said yes to it, as Paul soon makes clear.

In chapter eleven he confronts the problem of a community overflowing with "wisdom" and the gifts of the Spirit and yet have missed the point of the Eucharist. In a striking denunciation, reminiscent of Amos (I Cor 11:17) he says that they would be better off not celebrating together. They come together in disunity to celebrate the sign of unity.

Like Jesus, they still celebrated the Eucharist in the

Like Jesus, they still celebrated the Eucharist in the context of a meal, but it was a meal in which some went hungry because they were poor. The wealthier Corinthians thought nothing of sharing a bit of Eucharistic bread, and not sharing their daily bread. Ignoring the Body of Christ around the altar, they are all enthused at the Body of Christ on the altar.

Fir Paul this makes no sense. It is receiving unworthily and sinning against the Body and Blood of the Lord. "He who eats and drinks without recognizing THE BODY eats and drinks a judgment on himself" (11:29). When Paul wrote the Greek of this text, it seems that he left it intentionally ambiguous. In the previous chapter he has been talking about the use of freedom and love in the community, the Body of Christ. In the following chapter he deals with the charismata at the service of the community, the Body of Christ. He concludes with "You then are the Body of Christ" (I Cor 12:27).

For Paul "recognizing the Body" is both sacramental and ecclesial or communitarian. Great faith in the Eucharist is impossible without recognition of Jesus' real presence in his members. The Eucharist is the Body and the community is the Body. Piety which has no problem seeing the mystery beyond the common elements of bread and wine, but cannot see the mystery of Christ in common people, is no piety at all.

When Jesus said, "Do this in remembrance of me" (I Cor 11:24) he was referring not only to repeating words over bread and wine, but to the sharing of oneself in community. In John's Gospel where the washing of the feet is the action highlighted at the last supper, he uses similar words: "As I have done, so you must do" (Jn 13:15).

Our liturgy has changed a great deal in the last few years. Some of the mysteriousness has been taken away so that *the* mystery might become more evident. The signs have been made more clear and intelligible. But all of this was done, not to change the worship of the people, but to change the people who worship.

Communities which profess to be at the heart of the Church and living witnesses of the call of Jesus should manifest both the power and centrality of the liturgy in a striking way. The council has told us that the Eucharist is the source of the Church's life and the center to which all her activity is directed. These can remain just words in a Council document, or religious communities, one body because they all partake of the same bread, can show forth their truth.

11.

_____ THE POOR OF YAHWEH

The community of the Old Testament, by their very reporting of Abraham's vocation, showed their recognition that faith and life in covenant presuppose a spirit and actuality of poverty, at least in its beginnings. Abraham had to give up country, home and family, in order to become a pilgrim believer. However, they also expected that faith, far from making them poor, would materially enrich them. After all, in spite of what he gave up, Abraham and his descendants were promised the land, rich with milk and honey. For them, faith may have begun in poverty, but it was hardly to be lived in poverty.

After Moses, as the systems of laws developed, the conviction that God would not just care for his people, but would take care to make them prosperous became deeply imbedded in their religious thinking. Hearkening to the voice of the Lord became identified with obeying all the laws. This obedience was to be rewarded with riches and prosperity. The sign of the fidelity of God's people would be the size of their "bank account." "If you are careful to observe all his commandments which I enjoin on you today, the Lord, your God, will raise you high above all the nations of the earth . . . The Lord will open for you his rich treasure house of the heavens" (Dt 28:1,12).

These words, put in the mouth of Moses, many years after Israel had occupied the promised land, were a last ditch effort to recall a luke-warm people to fidelity. But since they were acting like children they were treated like children. "Be good and I'll give you some candy."

Unfortunately, the opposite was also perceived as true. Poverty must be God's punishment for disobedience. (If you don't behave, I'll take away your candy!) If a person were poor, it must obviously be a result, of his godlessness. Poverty was seen as an indication of Yahweh's righteous displeasure, if not his curse (Dt 28:15 ff.). While this rather simplistic view of retribution may have been necessary to encourage a primitive people, it became a dangerous point of view in times that should have grown more sophisticated in theology and spirituality.

Job's predicament shows that the traditional theology just did not correspond to experience. Like all simple solutions it raised more questions than it answered. Anticipating Calvin's predestination which could be used to justify the sweat shops of the industrial revolution, deuteronomic theology gave the rich the right to oppress the poor, since they were already cursed by God.

In a sense, poverty, considered a curse for nonobservance of the law, put one outside the community. It was the sign of excommunication. However, it was a nice, neat theory that just did not stand up under the facts. Many who knew themselves to be men of faith, also experienced great poverty. In fact, as had the poverty of their father Abraham their poverty also

led them to a deeper faith. In their absolute abandonment and need, they knew they could look for help
only to God. The rich, supposedly so because of their
piety, had nothing to give the poor but disdain. The
whole attitude of the religious leaders toward the
poor is summed up in John's Gospel in their attitude
toward the poor who turned to Jesus. "You do not
see any of the Sanhedrin believing in him, do you?
Or the Pharisees? Only this lot, that knows nothing
about the law—and they are lost anyway" (Jn 7:48,49)!
The poor were literally damned, cursed and unloved
by God.

But because their poverty led them to real faith,
the poor became a community within the community.
The word *anawim,* originally a term of approbrium
for the poor, on the lips of the prophets became a
term of praise for the faithful remnant, the true Israel.
By the poverty of their lives they witnessed to the
only treasure they had, God himself.

Far from being bearers of a curse, they alone became bearers of hope and promise in the midst of a
rich, proud and complacent people. *Anawim* came to
stand for humility and lowliness, as it is frequently
translated in English Bibles (cf. Zep 2:3; 3:11,12).

The prophets took up their cause, and became their
voice. "The afflicted and the needy seek water in vain,
their tongues are parched with thirst. I, the Lord, will
answer them; I, the God of Israel, will not forsake
them" (Is 41:17). And his very turning toward them
would be a sign of his presence among men: "That all
may see and know, observe and understand, that the
hand of the Lord has done this" (Is 41:20).

They had cried out. They were the people who called upon the name of the Lord, the people of prayer. In what an unexpected and marvelous way he would respond to their expectation and hope, they had no way of knowing. One day in Nazareth their prayers were answered, their hope fulfilled, beyond their wildest imaginings. In the synagogue Jesus read of that mysterious figure that Yahweh would send to them, the servant of the Lord.

"The spirit of the Lord is upon me;. therefore he has anointed me. He has sent me to bring glad tidings to the poor, to proclaim liberty to captives, recovery of sight to the blind and release to prisoners, to announce a year of favor from the Lord." Rolling up the scroll he gave it back to the assistant and sat down. All in the synagogue had their eyes fixed on him. Then he began by saying to them, "Today this Scripture passage is fulfilled in your hearing" (Lk 4:18-21).

Jesus was theirs, one of them. They were to be the first to receive the Good News. He was the embodiment of their spirit, already celebrated in song by his mother, the queen of the poor.

My being proclaims the greatness of the Lord, my spirit finds joy in God my savior, for he has looked upon his servant in her lowliness. He has shown might with his arm; he has confused the proud in their inmost thoughts. He has deposed the mighty from their thrones and raised the lowly to high places (Lk 1:46-48, 51,52).

And if this spirit of the *anawim* was a sign of hope and expectation in the Old Testament, it was to be the sign of fulfillment in the New. If it was characteristic of the mother who gave him birth, it was characteristic of all who found life in him. In their lives, it was to be a sign of the breaking in of the Kingdom. "How blest are the poor in spirit, the reign of God is theirs" (Mt 5:3).

That this was not just an attitude, but a spirit which was manifested in a life of real poverty is evident from Luke's reporting of Jesus' preaching. He understood it as having been addressed to those who were really poor. "Blest are you poor; the reign of God is yours (Lk 6:20). A real sign of the Kingdom is the open arms of those, who, uncluttered by wealth can reach out to the Lord. They manifest to all that they were willing to be possessed by nothing else or no one else, but the Lord.

Paul's statement of poverty is a *sine qua non* to an understanding of the power that possessed him. "I have come to rate all as loss, in the surpassing knowledge of my Lord Jesus Christ . . . All I want is to know Christ and the power flowing from his resurrection" (Phil 3:8-10).

Indeed, the early Christian community's meditation on the poverty of Christ, as given by Paul in the previous chapter of Philippians sees in it the very process and means of his redemptive work and ultimate exhaltation. Before the Incarnation, he was God apart, other, transcendent who, as in the Exodus, could have appeared among men in all his glory. He would have been immediately recognized by them.

Instead, he came the way of poverty, emptying himself, becoming the lowliest of the lowly, the poorest of the poor. He did not cling to what was his by right. Poverty was the way that he chose to call men to himself "to proclaim to the glory of God the Father: Jesus Christ is Lord" (Phil 2:11). But this proclamation of the Lordship of Jesus can only be done by those who have his attitude of poverty, for Paul prefaces whe whole of this passage with the injunction: "Your attitude must be that of Christ" (Phil 2:5).

The earliest Christian creed "Jesus is Lord," a statement of belief and commitment, can only be spoken and lived from the freedom of poverty. If he is Lord of my life, then there is nothing else that lords it over my life. If I am possessed by something or someone else, then, to that extent, I am not possessed by him. Far from being religious, I won't even be Christian.

In a generation preoccupied with wars on poverty, a poverty that dehumanizes man so that he cannot even think of anything but the needs of his stomach the proclamation of religious poverty may sound a bit odd. But he must have been thought a bit odd, too, when he proclaimed it as the first beatitude, and he doesn't seem to have changed his mind since.

12.

SINGLE FOR THE SAKE
_____ OF THE KINGDOM

If poverty was viewed in the Old Testament as being something less than a sign of God's concern, celibacy was considered to be alien to everything that a truly religious person stood for. Even the faith of the *anawim* would have been a bit shaken by the idea of remaining single. Later rabbis even went so far as to categorize it in terms of murder. It simply made no sense for it implied childlessness. And fundamental to the promises made to Abraham by God was the expectation of children. Celibacy would leave no room for the fulfillment of that promise, in which every pious Israelite hoped to participate.

The plight of both Hanna, the mother of Samuel (I Sm 1-2) and of Elizabeth the mother of the Baptist (Lk 1:5 ff.) illustrate the shame of being childless. This turn of fortune was bad enough, but how much worse it would have been for a person to have chosen freely not to have offspring.

This attitude, which left no room for celibacy right up until Christian times resulted from the fact that revelation of an after life was a latecomer on the stage of the Old Testament. Thus, except for a nebulous and uncertain existence in Sheol, God's people knew of no way to achieve immortality except in their children. One psalmist even tries to convince God that he should be cured from a fatal illness: "For among the dead no one remembers you; in the nether world (Sheol) who gives you thanks" (Ps 6:6 cf. also Ps 29:10)?

Death was the end, and childlessness meant total fading off into oblivion, without any hope whatwoever. There was even legislation in the Old Testament to provide that this calamity would befall no man. According to the Levirate law the community was to come to the rescue of the man who died childless (Dt 25:5 ff.). His nearest male relative was to perpetuate his name by having children for him by his widow. This is well illustrated in the charming story of Ruth and Boaz (cf. esp. Ruth 4:10).

Jesus Christ himself found such a union among his ancestors (cp. Gn 38:6 and Mt 1:3). His ancestress Tamar tricked her father-in-law Juda into having relations with her, when he refused to provide one of his other sons to raise up offspring in the name of her deceased husband. In the same episode the infamous Onan was slain, not because he spilled his seed, but because in interrupting relations with his sister-in-law he was refusing immortality to his brother.

Attitudes that gave rise to such a practice as the Levirate law hardly left room for celibacy. It would never have been appreciated as a sign of God's covenant love. Hosea's life shows that a loving married life was to be looked upon as a primary sign of the covenant. "I will espouse you to me forever; I will espouse you in right and justice, in love and in mercy (Hos 2:21).

As far as is known, the prophets themselves, ardent proclaimers of the covenant, and men with a one track

mind where it was concerned apparently saw no reason
to be celibate themselves (*cf.* Hos: Is 8:1-4; Ez 24:15ff.).
Jeremiah is the only exception. He is to be celibate
as a sign to the people (Jer 16:1-5). But his celibacy
is a voice that speaks to the community, not of love,
but of their own impending exile and loneliness. His
celibacy and childlessness were to be a sign of the
abandonment of the people by God. His vocation was
to symbolize covenant broken and life without God.

Jeremiah's prophetic sign of celibacy is not exactly
the sign we'd like celibacy to be today. It does, however, show that God may ask some to use their
lives as an unusual but prophetic sign, manifesting
his will to the rest of the community.

As is evident from Paul's teaching, the New Testament in no way lessens the value of marriage as a
sign to the community of covenant life with God.
"This is a great foreshadowing. I mean that it refers
to Christ and the church" (Eph 5:32). However, Jesus
with his revelation of the possibility of eternal life
with himself, also introduces celibacy as a distinct
charism within the Christian community. Thus, it
presupposes an intimate life with Jesus, hereafter, which
can only be, if one has lived intimately with him
here. "Eternal life is this: to know you, the only
true God, and him whom you have sent, Jesus Christ"
(Jn 17:3).

Jesus gives his teaching on celibacy in Matthew's
Gospel in the context of a reply that he makes to the
pharisees on the question of divorce.

I now say to you, whoever divorces his wife (lewd conduct is a separate case) and marries another commits adultery, and the man who marries a divorced woman commits adultery. His disciples said to him, "If that is the case between man and wife, it is better not to marry." He said, "Not everyone can accept this teaching, only those to whom it is given to do so. Some men are incapable of sexual activity from birth; some have been deliberately made so; and some there are who have freely renounced sex for the sake of God's reign. Let him accept this teaching who can" (Mt 19:9-12).

In verse ten, the disciples themselves introduce the possibility of celibacy, but only as a barely viable alternative to the burden of the indisolubility of marriage which he has just enunciated. Jesus responds to them by making three points about celibacy. First, it depends upon a call, and thus is a charism that is not given to everyone. Secondly, it is a free gift and must be accepted freely (unlike congenital impotency or forced castration). Finally, it is a way of life that is lived for the sake of the Kingdom.

Since Jesus does not elaborate on this, and the best commentary on the Bible is the Bible itself it will be helpful to examine the Matthean work of redaction, seeing how he has used this teaching of Jesus by looking at the context.

Unlike most of the teaching of Jesus, which is usually given at least by one other evangelist, this one is unique to Matthew. The teaching on marriage and divorce is paralleled in both Mk 10:2-15 and Lk 16:18 but neither follows it with the words of Jesus on celibacy. This is surprising especially for Luke's Gospel, written for gentile Chritians who would be inclined to give such teaching a hospitable reception. They were already familiar with religious celibates such as the vestal virgins. Thus its inclusion in the Gospel written for a community of Jewish Christians, with their Old Testament ideas about celibacy, makes it all the more startling.

It should be noticed also, that Matthew is repeating himself. He has already included the teaching on divorce in the Sermon on the Mount (5:32). Unless he is repeating it for emphasis, which is unlikely, since he doesn't repeat more important teachings of Jesus, its repetition must have been simply as a backdrop for the point that he really wanted to make: celibacy.

Matthew's Gospel is called the Gospel of the Church, not only because he is the only one of the four to use the word (16:18; 18:17) but because his writing frequently reflects and justifies practices and ways of life already in existence in the community at the time when he is writing, after 70 A.D. For example, the passage we are dealing with is immediately followed by Jesus' blessing of the children, a story told to justify the practice of infant baptism in the early community. It is not unlikely that the teaching on celibacy also reflects a way of life of some of the earliest members of the church.

Matthew's is a highly structured Gospel. He arranges the teachings of Jesus into five discourses (paralleling the five books of Moses). This passage introduces the last discourse which is concerned with the establishing of the Kingdom and only ends with its actual establishment by the passion and Resurrection of Jesus. Thus he gives celibacy an important role in Jesus' plan. In this section (Mt 19-25) it is joined to the teaching of Jesus on entering the Kingdom as a child, poverty that can only be lived with God's help, God's mercy, authority and service in the Kingdom, the law of love and teachings on the end times. Placing the teaching on celibacy in the company of all of these, Matthew obviously means to give it an important role in the extablishing of the Kingdom.

Writing over a decade earlier to the community of Corinth in which charismata flourished, Paul also refers to the charism of celibacy. He speaks of it to a people who were tending to view the body and sexuality as evil. According to one faction, the way to triumph over them was to give into temptations, then they wouldn't be bothersome (I Cor 6:12 ff.). Another faction was all for an asceticism that would supress sexual activity even among the married (7:1b is their supposition, not Paul's teaching).

Paul's reply (7:5) is, that for the married, temporary celibacy is justified only occasionally to allow time for prayer. He manifests a preference for celibacy but acknowledges that his own preferences are not to interfere with God's gifts, either to celibacy or marriage (7:7).

At this time (the present time of stress 7:26), Paul is much preoccupied with his belief in the imminent second coming of Christ. (I tell you, brothers, the time is short; 7:29.) Such a life would manifest to the community a sense of priorities, an overpowering concern for the things of the lord (7:34). Thus, for Paul, celibacy is not a disdaining of sexuality, but a gracious gift of God, given to some, that they may witness to the overpowering reality of Jesus Christ and his Kingdom and devote all their efforts to building it up.

However, like all gifts, it must be infused with the fundamental one of love. "If I give my body to be burned, but have not love, I gain nothing" (I Cor 13:3). It is a life of love not loneliness. If it excludes sexual activity, it does not exclude the emotional and psychological needs for affection and love which one has a right to expect in a celibate community. Jesus never said that the Kingdom would be built up by lonely, petty, small-minded people. It is built up by those who have a vision of a life of love in Jesus Christ and share that with the community, in the freedom that celibacy brings.

13.

If the concept of celibacy is not much in evidence in the Bible, obedience leaps from practically every page, since with faith, it is a correlative of covenant. It begins with the story of Adam and Eve, recounted by an inspired author shortly after the time of David in the tenth century before Christ. He describes the beginning, the fall of the first parents in terms of the sin that he saw around him in his own time.

He saw his people, still holding on to Yahweh as the God of the Exodus, but also turning toward the fertility gods of Canaan. As they emerged from being nomads to farmers, they began imitating the Canaanites in controlling the forces of fertility that were thought to rule the land. He saw them falling into the pagan practices of trying to control nature and fertility, and thus, the very forces of life itself. They would leave nothing to God, but take things in their own hands, trying to be like gods.

The story he tells in Genesis 2 and 3 has constant undercurrents of sexuality, because it was literally in fornicating with the temple prostitutes that the fertility cult was conducted. They hoped to awaken the interest of Baal and Astarte, the god of fertility and his consort, by participating in the sexual rites in the Canaanite sanctuaries. Just as it was the Canaanite

77

practices, whose phallic symbol was the serpent, which led them astray, so it is the serpent who sparks the disobedience of Adam and Eve. That is why he characterizes the punishment of Adam and Eve as being in their functions of sexuality and fertility. But in telling the story he sees the sin, not as one of sexuality, but of mankind's will to power. It is the tale of man's unwillingness to be anything less than "like gods." He always wants things his own way.

After describing the terrible ruptures brought into community by disobedience and assertion of one's will (e.g. Adam is ashamed in fromt of Eve; both flee from God; and Cain kills Abel.), the author introduces Abraham. In him, faith gives rise to obedience. He is in direct contrast to the first parents who put their faith in themselves and disobeyed. Abraham puts his faith in God and obeys. He becomes a seeker of the will of God instead of asserting himself and doing his own thing. In faith, he becomes a listener, a hearer.

Being somewhat of a primitive language, Hebrew frequently uses one word for which we require two in English. The Hebrew word *shamah* means both to listen and to obey. Always practical and concrete in his thinking, the Hebrew could never hear and say "so what." That would not really be hearing. Real hearing was effective; it entered into a person's life in a practical way, impelling him to do something about what he heard. He obeyed. He acted or reacted to the word that he heard. Thus, the posture of being a listener puts Abraham and all who are his children in direct contrast with Adam and Eve who found other voices to listen to than the Lord's.

True obedience follows from listening to the Lord who speaks, in the context of the community that he has brought together from their own Babel, to "hear his voice" (Ex 19). But the one obeying must search out that voice. And it is not always the voice that we expect to hear.

Elijah the prophet found this out the hard way (I Kgs 19). After an arduous forty day journey to Sinai where he wanted to hear the thundering voice of God whom he expected to be as angry as he was, he was surprised to hear the voice of the Lord in " a tiny whispering sound," or as it may be translated, "the voice of a whispering breeze."

Samuel, as a child, so ready to obey the voice that he heard in the calm and holiness of the temple, "speak, Lord for your servant is listening" (I Sm 3:10) was a bit more reluctant when Yahweh's voice was expressed in the clamorous voice of the people who wanted Samuel's powers transferred to a king (I Sm 8:22). Mysterious voices in the temple seem a bit easier to recognize as God's than the tumultuous ones in the community, but they may be no less valid. He had to learn as a superior that he had not cornered the market on God's voice or his will.

Then, even Saul, the king he annointed, had to learn a lesson in obedience (I Sm 15:22). The king thought he could remain on God's good side by abundant sacrifices.

But Samuel said: Does the Lord so delight in holocausts and sacrifices as in obedience to the command of the Lord? Obedience is better than sacrifice (I Sm 15:22).

Later, the prophets, independent of the structures of authority, were used as God's voice. (*Prophemi* means to speak on behalf of another). But hearing his voice, obeying him, became Israel's stumbling block. "When Israel was a child I loved him, out of Egypt I called my son. The more I called them, the farther they went from me" (Hos 11:1,2b). It is precisely this condemnation of the old Israel that Matthew transforms into a prophecy of the new Israel, Jesus Christ (Mt 2:15). The new Israel hears the call, he obeys. "Doing the will of him who sent me. . .is my food" (Jn 4:35).

He, knowing the real meaning of obedience, reserves his sternest words of condemnation for those whose boast was that they were obedient to the law. In the very process they subverted life, love and covenant without which law has no meaning (Mt 15). Obedience to law is not always obedience to God!

But if Christ's own attitude toward obedience far surpassed Israel's, like our own, it involved struggle and growth, as manifested in the agony in the garden. According to Hebrews 5:7,8 this was a process, not an isolated instance.

In the days when he was in the flesh, he offered prayers and supplications with loud cries, and tears to God, who was able to save him from death, and he was heard because of his reverence. Son though he was, he learned obedience from what he suffered (Heb 5:7,8).

If Jesus Christ is the model of obedience, he is also the model of the struggle that it entails. The obedience to death on a cross that brought about our salvation (Phil 2) is in the context of his acceptance of our weak humanity, without reserve, without escape clauses. His very becoming man is in contrast to the first man who tried to be like God. Obedience is the difference, as Paul makes clear in Romans 5:19.

However, the history of the primitive Christian community makes it evident that obedience may not simply be a yes to the structure of authority. Paul, in obedience to the Gospel and the freedom that it calls us to, withstood Peter to the face (Gal 2:11). Confrontation is an unpleasant task at any time, but if Paul had shied away from it, we might still be a sect of Judaism rather than the Body of Christ.

Even Paul recognized that he did not have the last word. "All of us who are spiritually mature must have this attitude. If you see it another way, God will clarify the difficulty for you" (Phil 3:15). God might speak with other voices than his own.

And the same apostle who was responsible for establishing so much of the structure of the primitive Church, insisted in the very first Christian document that we have (ca. 51 A.D.):

We beg you, brothers, respect those among you whose task it is to exercise authority in the Lord and admonish you; esteem them with the greatest love because of their work . . . Remain at peace with one another. Do not stifle the spirit. Do not despise prophecies. Test everything; retain what is good (Thes 5:12,13 and 19-21).

Since obedience is hearing, Paul was concerned about the voice that was heard. Personal impulse may produce rumblings, but they are not to be confused with the voice of God. "You know that when you were pagans you were led astray to mute idols as impulse drove you" (I Cor 12:3).

Whether the voice of the Lord calls through the superior, the community, a prophet, or myself, it must be listened to and discerned. The alternatives are a return to either pharisaism or egotism. The Gospel is a call to listen and to obey, but in the context of freedom and loving service.

My brothers, remember that you have been called to live in freedom—but not a freedom that gives free rein to the flesh. Out of love, place yourselves at one another's service. The whole law has found its fulfillment in this one saying: "You shall love your neighbor as yourself" (Gal 5:13,14).

14.

AUTHORITY, _____GIFT TO THE COMMUNITY

The name of God, Yahweh, as revealed to Moses in the burning bush (Ex 3), comes from the Hebrew word "to be." In revealing his name, however, God was not indicating that he was abstract, impersonal being. Hebrew is not capable of such a translation. Rather he was revealing, "I am, who am with you, always present to you, never leaving you in isolation or helpless." Thus his name is the promise of what he will be, the guiding force and leader of his people. He will always be there to call them forth to himself, from whatever slavery they find themselves in.

He thus sets the pattern for authority and leadership. It has one purpose, to lead from slavery (no people) to covenant community (my people) (Hos 2:1).

This was the role he gave to Moses, who was such a reluctant but effective leader. Several practical aspects of Moses' pioneering role emerge from the book of Exodus. He is above all, a reluctant leader, very much aware of his own weakness and inability to perform the task. This nervousness arose from his own false understanding of what it meant to exercise authority. He conceived it as a function he had to perform by himself, even though God had revealed himself as Yahweh, "I am who am" with you. "I will be with you" (Ex 3:12). But self-conscious of the image he would give as a poor speaker, Moses begged off. "If you please, Lord, send someone else. Then the Lord became angry with Moses and said: Have you not your brother Aaron, the Levite" (Ex 4:13)? As superior, Moses did not have to stand in isolation with the world on his shoulders. There were others to help him.

But besides being slow of speech, he was also slow to learn. He developed a tendency of thinking that he knew best, and no one could make decisions but himself. He had to be involved in and control all the petty affairs of the community (Ex 18:13 ff.). His father-in-law had to tell him that his role was to have a broader vision, manifesting God's will and showing the people how they were to live in covenant. Other members of the community could take care of lesser activities. Such petty involvement by himself could only infringe upon his true role of leadership.

Moses showed here a willingness to take advice, and to change as the needs of the community indicated. This, of course, arose from the fundamental attitude of his faith, as a passover person, willing to move off into the unknown. Without that, the Hebrews would have remained in Egypt, and never become a community. His leadership was a gift to them.

One of the roles that Moses perceives as intrinsic to his authority is praying for the community. He constantly goes before God seeking his will for them. He leads them to respond to God's call (Ex 19). He spells out the demands of Covenant life (Ex 20). He helps them to celebrate their identity as God's people in the liturgy (Ex 24). All of this followed time spent with God in prayer. His periods of forty days with the Lord set the pattern for our own Lenten practice.

Moses was not afraid to show strength when the covenant was threatened (Ex 32), but even then a delightful dialogue of prayer between God and himself is reported. The Lord is fed up with his people, and the author has Moses convincing Yahweh how silly he'll look to the Egyptians, if he doesn't live up to his name. Moses' prayer, as well as his anger arise from one source. He does not brood over their disloyalty to him, or rejectionn of his leadership. He is angry because what they have done has injured covenant and community in which he is totally absorbed.

Following Moses' death, and the passing of Josue, his successor, authority was shared and ceased to be in the hands of one man. Only in times of crisis, in the long period of the Judges, did one man assume a central and charismatic role as leader. But no community can live from crisis to crisis, and so in the time of Samuel, the last Judge, a cry arose for a king, lest the community fall into chaos, and be destroyed.

The more conservative party did not want this change, giving authority into the hands of one person. They felt that they had done well enough without it, and as Samuel indicated, such central authority could itself be destructive of community. Thus two groups, equally interested in the community and the best way to live their life with God, were polarized over what structure was best suited to achieve it. (Cf. Jgs 21:24: a plea for release from the chaos of everyone doing as they pleased, and the opposite point of view in I Samuel 8: a post factum description of how superiors act when they put themselves above the community.)

The liberal faction wins, and Saul is annointed king. It is David, however, guileless, if not always guilt-less, who becomes *the* annointed one (*messiah*). He personifies all the future hopes for a *messiah* who would truly be a leader of God's people.

His son, Solomon, renowned as a wise man, had the insight to ask of the Lord that gift that is so neces-sary for every superior, *leb shomeah*, a listening heart (I Kgs 3:9).

His successors, messiahs all, were not noted, how-ever, for having hearts that listened to either God or man. They were preoccupied with themselves and their own enrichment. It was in this leadership vac-uum that prophecy arose. God was faithful even if his messiahs were not. The loud voices of the prophets rose above the weak voices of the kings.

Finally in the midst of leaders that had no time for him, there arose a great prophet. "They were spell-bound by his teaching, for his words had authority" (Lk 4:32). They had been so used to the nit picking of their pharisaic leaders who conceived of authority only in terms of enforcing laws that Jesus stood out be-cause of his vision and conviction.

He knew that men were more important than laws, even the God-given law of the sabbath (Lk 6). He refused to get bogged down in their petty discussions or legal arguments. He would not play their silly game of disputation on the relative importance of laws. He cut right through their jargon and recalled them to a vision of love.

When the Pharisees heard that he had silenced the Sadducees, they assembled in a body; and one of them, a lawyer, in an attempt to trip him up, asked him, "Teacher, which commandment of the law is the greatest?" Jesus said to him: "'You shall love the Lord your God with your whole heart, with your whole soul, and with all your mind.' This is the greatest and first commandment. The second is like it: 'You shall love your neighbor as yourself.' On these two commandments the whole law is based, and the prophets as well" (Mt 22:34–40).

His authority was his ability to show people the reality of God's call. It can hardly be said that the Gospels picture him as a lawyer, lawgiver, or enforcer of the law. Rather, time and again the Gospels indicate his word and example to those whom he entrusted the gift of authority in the Church. They were to be men of love in service to each other. The washing of the feet was followed by:

Do you understand what I just did for you? You address me as 'Teacher' and 'Lord,' and fittingly enough, for that is what I am. But if I washed your feet—I who am Teacher and Lord— then you must wash each other's feet (Jn 13:13,14).

Time and again, the image of Jesus as authority and leader, leaps from the Gospels. He is the shepherd who gives his life for the sheep, the servant, who knew of no greater love than to lay down his life for his friends.

Religious life today is in a process of experimenting with structures of authority. It finds itself in the company of the early community, to whom Jesus gave little in the way of detailed organization. Church order in the New Testament emerges in many forms and varied models for authority to be exercised in community. But whatever the structure of authority and leadership, they found no better way for it to function than following the example of the Lord. It is not likely that we can do any better.

15.

The tension that rose within the Old Testament community can be visualized even today in the social notice of a synagogue. One line will mention that there will be a meeting of the B'nai Berith, the Sons of the Covenant, the Jewish men's organization. The next line will announce that a teenager will become a full fledged member of the community by making his Bar Mitzvah, Son of the Commandment or Son of the law. The relation between covenant and law was an important issue in the Old Testament as well as in the primitive Christian community (and in the Church today)!

Covenant is not law. Covenant is relationship, community. Law is the spelling out of the demands of such a relationship. It prohibits those things that will weaken the relationship, and commands those things which will strengthen it. Mature people, people of strong faith, do not need law. Their total commitment to covenant tells them what will be good or bad for the relationship. For example, husbands and wives don't need legislation to tell them how they should act toward each other. Love tells them. Abraham himself was given no law to tell him how to act in covenant. Faith told him.

The law only came hundreds of years later with

89

Moses, and the very historical situation that gave rise to the commandments and law codes show what kind of people need law. In many ways the hebrews were a primitive people. Hosea is not off the mark when he calls them children. "When Israel was a child, I loved him, out of Egypt I called my son. The more I called them, the farther they went from me" (Hos 11:1,2).

Children are self-willed and have to have the law laid down to them until they mature and know how to act. But, "Do this" and "Don't touch that," when addressed to a twenty-one year old indicates a serious problem!

Law is also necessary for those whose relationship and grasp of covenant is weak. Obeying laws can lead to an understanding of the purpose of the law, and thus to a grasp of covenant, the only reason for the law's existence. Moses saw how weak his people were. No sooner had he announced the covenant in Exodus 19, and celebrated it in the liturgy of Exodus 24 than they built the golden calf, led by Aaron.

With that, the Lord said to Moses, "Go down at once to your people, who you brought out of the land of Egypt, for they have become depraved. They have soon turned aside from the way I pointed out to them, making for themselves a molten calf and worshiping it, sacrificing to it and crying out, 'This is your God, O Israel, who brought you out of the land of Egypt!' I see how stiff-necked this people is," continued the Lord to Moses (Ex 32:7–9).

If they were ever to learn what covenant meant, they needed laws. "You shall not make for yourselves molten gods" (Ex 34:17). By excluding other covenants, they might come to a realization of what life with Yahweh meant.

Law is also necessary as communities grow larger. (There is no evidence that the eleven apostles sensed a great urge to produce a code of law right after the Ascension.) When Exodus 12:37 ff. mentions, with some exaggeration, that six-hundred thousand men on foot, not counting children, left Egypt along with a crowd of mixed ancestry, it is a reference not only to quantity of manpower, but quality of covenant commitment. Their behavior in the desert indicates there was great difference among them as far as their willingness to live out a covenant life with Yahweh and each other. Communities will always show such variations in the maturity and commitment of the members, and laws become necessary for the common good, even though the mature are not in need of them.

Law has its own dangers however. The most serious is that it can replace covenant, without which it has no meaning. Religion then becomes legal observance rather than covenant life in community. Response is based on fear of breaking the law rather than faith working through love. Worst of all, the One who calls is eventually perceived, not as the loving God, Yahweh, ever with us, but as the Divine Policeman ever on the watch for law breakers. (Or, "Ambush Theology" as it has been called!) It is no accident that many, unfamiliar with the total Old Testament, and knowing only its repetitious commandments and laws, have caricatured the God of the Old Testament as a God of anger. The heretic Marcion went so far as to teach that there were two different Gods, the Old Testament God of anger and the New Testament God of love.

It was Jesus' great contribution that he cut through the legalism and return to the law of love (Mt 22:37ff.). But in doing this he was going back to the very roots of covenant. His words about love of God and neighbor were quotations from the Old Testament (Dt 6:5; Lv 19:18). They are startling on his lips only because they had been so buried under legalism. His praise of the publican who sought covenant love rather than the pharisee, the professional religious and observer of the law, could not make his own attitude any clearer (Lk 18:9ff.).

The law, which had been given as a means to express covenant relationship became an end in itself. Thus did lawyers become the religious leaders and pharisees the holy ones to be emulated.

Law can only affect external observance, as Jesus well knew when he condemned the pharisees throughout the Gospels, but especially in Mt 23 for being frauds, blind guides and whitewashed tombs. And they thought they were being religious! The worst of it was that they were the leaders, the yeast that should cause the community to rise and grow. "Be on the lookout against the yeast of the Pharisees and Saducees" (Mt 16:6). The disciples, feeling that Jesus was a bit harsh on the religious leaders, told him that the pharisees were scandalized by what he said. He backed up not at all, for his little community must be formed well if they were to lead his people. "Let them go their way; they are blind leaders of the blind. If one

blind man leads another, both will end in a pit"
(Mt 15:14).

Small wonder that we do not find Jesus legislating
in the Gospels. Matthew, on the Mount, depicts him
as the new Moses, but not the law giver. Jesus tries
to get into the heart of man and change him from
within. The Beatitudes and the entire Sermon on the
Mount are not the words of a legislator, but one who
calls to love.

But even with all this, it took a long time for Jesus'
community to understand what he meant. After Pentecost, Peter still thought that one had to become a
law abiding Jew to become a Christian. Not once or
twice, but three times did he need to have the vision
of the non-kosher food to realize that he was not the
leader of a sect of the Jews (Acts 10:9ff.).

I begin to see how true it is that God shows no partiality.
Rather, the man of any nation who fears God and acts up-
rightly is acceptable to him. This is the message he has sent
to the sons of Israel, the good news of peace proclaimed through
Jesus Christ who is the Lord of all (Acts 10:34–36).

If Peter "began to see," others in the Jewish Christian community did not. Known as Judaizers, they
began to follow in the steps of St. Paul, but not in
his spirit. His constant preoccupation with the freedom from the law that we have in Jesus Christ (Phil
3, Gal, Rom 7, Col 2:16, and I Tm 1), shows what a
real problem this was in the early Church. His most
extensive treatment of the theme is found in Galatians.

As everywhere, he had preached in Galatia the one

Gospel revealed to him by Jesus himself. "I assure you, brothers, the gospel I proclaimed to you is no mere human invention. I did not receive it from any man, nor was I schooled in it. It came by revelation from Jesus Christ" (Gal 1:11,12). The Good News is this:

It was through the law that I died to the law, to live for God. I have been crucified with Christ, and the life I live now is not my own; Christ is living in me. I still live my human life, but it is a life of faith in the Son of God, who loved me and gave himself for me. I will not treat God's gracious gift as pointless. If justice is available through the law, then Christ died to no purpose (Gal 2:19–21)!

The Judaizers (whom he tells to go to hell! 1:7–9) were preaching another version, their own, of the Gospel: salvation is a two track process, faith in Christ *and* in the law. Both are necessary for life. Paul knew the rabbinical teaching that law could give men life (Neh 9:29) but after his experience in Christ, he knew it to be false. If man could find life by his own efforts, obeying laws, then God was seriously mistaken. He need not have sent his gracious gift in Jesus Christ.

After showing that the Christian community is really the authentic community of Abraham, who came to life in God's love and received a blessing for his community 430 years before the law was even heard of, Paul explains the true function of the law.

It acts like a guardian for children who do not receive their inheritance until they grow up (4:1ff.). The message is clear: "Grow up." In the original meaning of the word, the law is the pedagogue, the monitor, who takes the child by the hand, helps him across the dangerous thoroughfares and brings him to the teacher (3:23ff.). Then the pedagogue retires, no longer necessary.

Paul's anger at those demanding circumcision, symbolic of the whole law, could not be more graphically expressed (5:12)! Being accused of watering down the Gospel so he could get more converts by making the Gospel easier for them, was more than he could take.

But Judaism did have this advantage. The law always let you know what God wanted you to do. Now, how would you know? Paul's reply is, that you have your choice. You can live a life directed by the flesh (*sarx*, selfish you) (5:16ff.). Or, you can live in the Spirit (5:22). Both will show their results, but for Christians there is only one way. ·

Those who belong to Christ Jesus have crucified their flesh with its passions and desires. Since we live by the spirit, let us follow the spirit's lead (Gal 5:24,25).

The recent past in the Church and religious life show indications that we had not learned from this history of the early Church. When law, whether Canon or the rule of religious communities is looked upon as a source of holiness, almost as sacramental, then we desperately need the maturity that Paul calls us to in Christian freedom. "The law of the spirit, the spirit of life in Christ Jesus, has freed you from the law of sin and death" (Rom 8:2).

16.

FREEDOM
_____ AND IDENTITY CRISIS

The medieval scholastics had an axiom: *agere se-quitur esse*. Every being acts according to its nature. Hundreds of years before, the prophets had already realized this. The people were acting the way they were, because they had forgotten what they were. While the prophets condemn their activity, it is in the context of trying to bring them back to a realization of their vocation. To get them to stop their activity would have only healed the symptom. The disease struck deep inside them. "Can the Ethiopian change his skin? The leopard his spots? As easily would you be able to do good, accustomed to evil as you are" (Jer 13:23).

Among the prophets the conviction arises that talking to Israel about life in covenant was like talking to a stone. So jaded and self-satisfied had the people become, that the prophets found that they were no longer communicating with them on the same wave length. It would be like talking to a five times divorced movie star about the indisolubility of marriage. "Their deeds do not allow them to return to their God; for the spirit of harlotry is in them, and they do not recognize the Lord" (Hos 5:4). They had an identity crisis. If they realized who they were, they would not be acting the way they were.

Ezechiel sees that the wound cannot be cured with bandaids. Nothing less than a heart transplant will suffice.

I will sprinkle clean water upon you to cleanse you from all your impurities, and from all your idols I will cleanse you. I will give you a new heart and place a new spirit within you, taking from your bodies your stony hearts and giving you natural hearts (Ez 36:25,26).

This ideal community, also spoken of by Jeremiah (31:31ff.) would consist of those who would be totally renewed, reborn in water and the spirit, as Jesus told Nicodemus (Jn 3:5). Then, they would know how to act, because they would have a consciousness of what God had accomplished in them. Hopefully!

Paul, however, found the situation not so idealistic as we sometimes imagine it. He found out that if man can be defined as a creature who remembers, he is also a creature who forgets. At least in Corinth he found people who remembered what they wanted to hear, and forgot the rest.

He had preached to them the same Gospel as he had in Galatia. In the Gospel we have been given the gift of freedom from the law, that living by the spirit, we might follow the spirit's lead (Gal 5:25). They only heard "Freedom." They forgot that the gift of Jesus is freedom to be a new creation and act accordingly. "All that matters is that one is created anew. Peace and mercy on all who follow this rule of life" (Gal 6:15).

But many who heard Paul's proclamation of the Gospel of Christian freedom took this to mean doing

as they pleased, doing their own thing, in the worst
sense of the expression. In a culture where philosophy
was an exercise in speculation (Acts 17:21) to satisfy
curiousity, and had little to do with the practical
affairs of day to day living, it became easy for the
Greek converts to transfer this attitude to Christianity.
One could think as a Christian and act as nature dic-
tates. Paul opposes this attitude:

The Spirit we have received is not the world's spirit but God's
Spirit, helping us to recognize the gifts he has given us. We
speak of these, not in words of human wisdom but in words
taught by the Spirit, thus interpreting spiritual things in spiritual terms. The natural man does not accept what is taught
by the Spirit of God. For him, that is absurdity. He cannot
come to know such teaching because it must be appraised in
a spiritual way. The spiritual man, on the other hand, can
appraise everything (I Cor 2:12-15b).

Otherwise they would be ensnared in the same trap
that had caught the people of the Old Testament.
They claimed they knew God and then acted as pagans.

Brothers, the trouble was that I could not talk to you as spiritual men but only as men of flesh, as infants in Christ. I fed
you with milk, and did not give you solid food because you
were not ready for it, you are not ready for it even now, being
still very much in a natural condition. For as long as there are
jealousy and quarrels among you, are you not of the flesh?
And is not your behavior that of ordinary men (I Cor 3:1-3)?

But they were not ordinary men, and if they had a
sense of their own identity, they would act according-

ly. *Agere sequitur esse,* but for Christians it requires an awareness of what Christ has made them to be. Confronted with this dichotomy in what they were, and how they were acting, Paul had to continue to confront the question of Christian freedom. After all, it was Paul himself who told them it was their gift.

What was wrong with a man, gifted with the freedom of the Gospel, sleeping with his step-mother (I Cor 5:1ff.)? What was wrong in sueing fellow Christians in pagan courts (6:1ff.)? What was wrong in giving in to one's sexual appetites, just as one satisfied his appetite for food (6:13ff.)? If there is no law then, "Everything is lawful for me." But Paul answers this ". . . but that does not mean that everything is good for me. Everything is lawful for me — but I will not let myself be enslaved by anything" (6:12). What good is freedom from the slavery to the law, if I allow myself to become a slave of my own passion and egoism?

In view of these terrible abuses in Corinth, Paul could have reneged on Gospel freedom and said that the time for experimentation is over. "You showed yourselves too immature to use your freedom. Back to the law."

But Paul never gave into the temptation to solve the problem of immaturity by a return to law. He knew that you don't get people to grow by treating them as children. That's what the law does.

You get people to grow by convincing them of what Christ has called them to be. When they realize that, they'll know how to act. To this community in which the worst depravity and excess was simply a way of life among both pagan and Christian, Paul never says you shouldn't do that because it's against the law. He says you wouldn't be doing that if you knew what you were. For the Christian it is beside the point that fornication is illegal or immoral. It is joining oneself to the body of a prostitute in total oblivion that one is a member of the body of Christ. "Do you not see that your bodies are members of the Body of Christ." (6:15) If there is any other reason for a Christian to be moral, Paul cannot think of it, except the realization of what makes him Christian. "You must know that your body is a temple of the Holy Spirit who is within—the spirit you received from God. You are not your own. You have been purchased, and at a price, so glorify God in your body" (6:9,20).

There is a strange and wonderful contrast in this epistle. It manifests a community going off the deep end, acting lewdly, even viciously, in the name of Christian freedom. At the same time it includes some of the most beautiful New Testament descriptions of what a Christian is. Paul knew that people will act as you expect them to act. Expect them to act as children, treating them thus, and they'll live up to your expectations. Paul always described his expectations of them in terms of what it meant to be a mature Christian. "You are God's cultivation, his building" (3:9).

Are you not aware that you are the temple of God, and that the Spirit of God dwells in you? If anyone destroys God's temple, God will destroy him. For the temple of God is holy, and you are that temple. All things are yours, whether it be Paul, or Apollos, or Cephas, or the world, or life, or death, or the present, or the future: all these are yours, and you are Christ's, and Christ is God's (I Cor 3:16,17; 3:21b-23).

This is the way to get people to act like Christians. Paul had no illusions. To return to life based on law is a step backward from Christ. *Agere sequitur esse.* But realize what the *"esse"* is. It is Christ in you. The source and center of our activity should tell us that:

Is not the cup of blessing we bless a sharing in the blood of Christ? And is not the bread we break a sharing in the body of Christ? Because the loaf of bread is one, we, many though we are, are one body, for we all partake of the one loaf (I Cor 10:16,17).

Besides those in the community who were guilty of the more obvious and flagrant abuses of freedom, there were some whose problem was more subtle, and they seemed to have the right on their side. They thought that their problem was simply a dietetic one (Ch. 8ff.). The pagan priests in Corinth had cornered the market on meat and all animals were sacrificed to idols before they were sold in the markets. The mature, knowledgeable (8:1), Christian knew that idols were nothing and so he had a right to enjoy his steak, no matter by whom or how it was prepared.

Paul agreed with them but was concerned for the new convert who would see his fellow Christians eating meat offered to idols and begin to think that it was alright to "think" as a Christian but continue to act in a day to day way as a pagan, in eating habits and other things as well. It was the very viewpoint that gave rise to the flagrant pagan living already mentioned. But this was far more subtle. Which should give way, the "right" and freedom of the mature Christian, or the weak faith of the other? Paul has no hesitation in affirming by the example of his own life (Ch. 9) that freedom is not the only principle that guides activity in the community. When it clashes with love and concern even for a brother who should know better, then freedom gives way.

Because of your "knowledge" the weak one perishes, that brother for whom Christ died. When you sin thus against your brothers and wound their weak consciences, you are sinning against Christ. Therefore, if food causes my brother to sin I will never eat meat again, so that I may not be an occasion of sin to him. You may ask, Why should my liberty be restricted by another man's conscience? And why is it, if I partake thankfully, that I should be blamed for the food over which I gave thanks? The fact is, that whether you eat or drink—whatever you do—you should do all for the glory of God (I Cor 8:11-13); 10:29b-31).

For communities that are coming to grips with emergence from whatever legalism and immaturity may have plagued them in the past, the new realization of Gospel freedom will present the same problems as it did at Corinth. But these problems are not solved by going back, or even yearning for "the good old days." These are the good new days of life in Christian freedom. But we'll only know how to live it if we follow Paul and encourage each other to realize what we are. That is the only identity crisis that counts.

17.

_____DOING YOUR OWN THING

One of the most ambiguous phrases to have entered into the la iguage of the post conciliar Curch is "Doing your own thing." Depending upon who is speaking, it can refer to a selfish lack of concern for the community, or to the demand of Jesus himself to use our talents. On the lips of some it is applied to the member of the community who is "different," whether in life-style, or apostolate or both. Unfortunately, it is a label that can be applied to the most generous of individuals who see structure as a means, not an end, as well as to one who is oblivious, if not disdainful of his roots and the community in which he found his identity in the first place. It is used as a threat against those who refuse to function as a "warm body" in one of the "traditional" apostolates of a community, and a battle cry by those who claim to have a broader, prophetic, vision of community and service.

Its emergence into our vocabulary may be recent, but it is an indication of the tension that begins on the first pages of the Bible. Throughout the history of God's call, this tension between individual and community has been lived out either in egoistic selfishness or loving generosity, but it has never been resolved.

In the garden of Eden we find Adam and Eve doing their own thing, forgetting that they were in covenant with God, and that covenant was their "thing." The near-destruction of community was the result.

An Israeli company publishes a clever tabloid, reporting Biblical events as if they were the news of the day. The first issue, published in Haran, editorializes about Abraham doing his own thing! From their point of view he was. Even the Bible portrays him as the unique individual who stands out, willing to change, go forth and believe (Gen 12). He found that God's thing was his thing, but how could he explain it to his friends?

Moses found himself an exile for doing something for the community, getting rid of an Egyptian oppressor (Ex 2:11). That put him on his guard against getting his fingers burned again. He didn't want to be accused of doing his own thing. "But Moses said to God, "Who am I that I should go to Pharaoh and lead the Israelites out of Egypt" (Ex 3:11). If Moses had continued to be paralyzed into inactivity by fear of being labeled as one who was doing his own thing, the covenant community would have remained but a dream.

Later on, it becomes evident that the more structured a community becomes and the more detailed are its laws, then anyone who emerges out of the flock, looks like a willful and stuborn sheep. Yet it may be in just such circumstances that people who are "different" are needed. When man has boxed in God and his activity and decided how he should

act among men, then charismatic figures are most
needed to show that our God sends his Spirit, like
the wind, blowing where it wills (Jn 3:8).

The prophets were always the victims of the sus-
picions of the establishment. Why couldn't God get
organized, and work through the proper channels?
People would be confused if they were called to
follow men without the proper credentials. Amos was
told by the ecclesiastical authority that he ought to
get a job like other self-respecting prophets had done,
and stop disturbing the community (Am 7:10 ff.).
But he knew that the false prophets were precisely
those charismatic voices of God, who stopped doing
their own thing and who had allowed themselves to
be institutionalized and co-opted by the community.

If there ever was one who was accused of doing
his own thing and upsetting the community, it was
Jesus. On the other hand, Judas, too, emerges as a
person who does his own thing. But he was interested
in the income for himself, while Jesus was preoccupied
with the outcome for all of mankind. "Doing the will
of him who sent me, and bringing his work to com-
pletion is my food" (Jn 5:34). The leaders of the time
had religion so well organized, that they readily
showed which of the two they preferred. They had even
decided where God could send prophets from. "Look
it up. You will not find the Prophet coming from
Galilee" (Jn 7:52).

The only time they will admit that Jesus, in doing
his own thing, is really doing the community's thing,
is when John has Caiphas saying more than he in-
tends.

Can you not see that it is better for you to have one man die (for the people) than to have the whole nation destroyed? (He did not say this on his own. It was rather as high priest for that year that he prophesied that Jesus would die for the nation—and not for this nation only, but to gather into one all the dispersed children of God.) (Jn 11:50-52)

This tension in the life of Jesus about being himself and what the community wanted him to be rises not only from his enemies, but also his disciples. The community's expectations of the messiah, enunciated by Peter, were a mold into which he refused to be poured (Mk. 8:33).

In addition to teaching that all will be held responsible for the use of their talents (Lk 19:11ff.), he also insisted that his followers might well take a lesson in initiative from the enterprising of this world (Lk 16:8).

Paul's own experience in using his talents in the primitive Christian community shows that not all the members heard the words of Jesus about talent and initiative. The first meeting with the disciples in Jerusalem, after his conversion, brought forth fear (Acts 8:23). His stock seems to have gone up when he showed a talent for taking care of the collection plate (Acts 11:27ff.; 12:25). But they did seem to breathe a sigh of relief when he was away from Jerusalem on his missionary journeys, "doing his own thing." That only lasted until some found out that "his own thing" was preaching a Gospel freed of circumcision and the law. It was only after a chapter of renewal (Acts 15; Gal 2) on that question that he was vindicated. They finally admitted that he had not been doing his own thing.

Following this episode in Acts there is an interesting occurrence. Paul and Barnabas disagree on whether John Mark (possibly the author of Mark's Gospel) who had dropped out before, should now come along on their "experimental apostolate." They agreed to disagree, and each went his separate way, doing his own thing in the name of the Lord.

Paul's own experience of suspicion and mistrust in the early community made him more tolerant, and a bit wary of accusing anyone of doing his own thing, unless it was incompatible with the Gospel. Besides, his own experience of the Lord had been so startling and unusual; who was he to say that he now had a detailed catalogue of all the ways in which the Lord might manifest himself? His own experience of Judaism helped him to know better than most what stagnation permeates a community in which everyone is stereotyped. He whose claim to be an apostle had been challenged because of a different life style (I Cor 9) was not about to burden others with the same pettiness, because they were "different."

If he saw himself as the Apostle of Christian Freedom, he knew that it was not just *from* the strictures of the law. It was a freedom *for* each member of the community to grow and discern his own charism. Any community bound together by the fundamental charism of love should be able to help its members discern their own gifts, and not tolerate diversity, but love it, as the legitimate manifestation of th Spirit. Paul describes how this love is manifested. "Love is patient, love is kind, love is not jealous." But the individual must remember, too: "Love is never rude, it is not self-seeking, it is not prone to anger, neither does it brood over injuries" (I Cor 13:4,5). And that "To each person the manifestation of the Spirit is given for the common good" (I Cor 12:7).

The tension between individual and community is no accident. It was intended as part of the human condition by the Lord who loved it so much he took it upon himself. When it is grounded in a love that is constantly amazed at the many splendored ways in which God manifest his power, it need not be a polarizing, deadening experience.

Needless to say, charismata and community are both of God, and only individuals and communities of prayer, seeking his will, and alive with his Spirit, wi'l avoid the pitfall of doing their own thing.

And may that phrase, and the spirit of all the phrases that label people and polarize them, through the mercy of God, rest in peace!

18.

THE PROPHETIC VOCATION

As is true even today, the word prophet in the old testament was applied to many different kinds of people. Moses, either because of some speech defect or simply a lack of eloquence, felt incapable of communicating with Pharaoh. "The Lord answered him, 'See! I have made you as God to Pharaoh, and Aaron your brother shall act as your prophet. You shall tell him all that I command you. In turn, your brother Aaron shall tell Pharaoh to let the Israelites leave his land" (Ex 7:1x2).

This becomes the classical pattern for prophecy. It is the role of men, whose word is not their own, but God's. That word is a call to liberation from whatever Pharaoh they find enslaving them so that they might begin their journey to covenant with God. The prophetic word is an invitation to *pesah* (Heb.: leap) or passover. It is a call to pass over from whatever hinders covenant, whether within themselves or outside, and to leap into the loving arms of their God.

During the course of the history of God's people, however, the word was applied to such diverse activities as being an old testament St. Anthony (cf. Samuel's finding the lost asses, I Sm 9:9) or entering a mystical state of union with God (I Sm 10:10; 19:24). However, Nathan, calling David to repentence for his sin with Bathsheba and the murder of her husband, is more typical of the later classical prophets, whose words have been preserved for us.

Unlike the folklore about Elijah and Elisha, recounted in the book of Kings, the lives of the later prophets manifest nothing startling. Hosea is the victim of an unhappy marriage. Amos is a migrant worker. Isaiah is of noble family, a member of the inner circles of the court. Jeremiah is a teenager, and Ezekiel is a priest. No pattern emerges by which they can be categorized or recognized.

They offer no great miracles to prove that they are from God. Their only credentials are the unfailing personal conviction that the word they speak is not their own, but God's, and that their lives, even before they speak, are examples of what God calls men to. If they are enthusiasts, then it must be in the original meaning of the word: *en theos*, in God. They were enthusastic because they were in God, in his covenant.

And from that vantage point, they saw things differently than other men. A prophetic figure himself, the recently deceased Rabbi Abraham Joshua Heschel, defined prophecy as exegesis (interpretation) of existence from a divine perspective. The prophet was able to discern what was going on around him with the vision of God, not the myopic view of man.

With this inherent sense of what was consonant with covenant and what was not, the prophet was like a musician with perfect pitch. It really is almost like a physical pain when he hears anything off key. But that vision and pitch springs from a life that is totally taken up into God. This explains the reaction of Isaiah, when, in a mystical state in the temple, he becomes acutely aware of the holiness of God and his own distance from it.

Then I said, Woe is me, I am doomed! For I am a man of unclean lips, living among a people of unclean lips; yet my eyes have seen the King, the Lord of hosts. Then one of the seraphim flew to me, holding an ember which he had taken with tongs from the altar. He touched my mouth with it. "See," he said, "now that this has touched your lips, your wickedness is removed, your sin purged." Then I heard the voice of the lord saying, "Whom shall I send? Who will go for us?" "Here I am," I said, "send me" (Is 6:5–8)!

His cleansing and his sending were the work of God. They are two sides of one coin. The awareness of the love of God, brings an awareness of the lack of it among men, and he must do something about it.

No prophet, however, sought out or welcomed such a thankless job. Amos would have much preferred to stay as a migrant worker, "a shepherd and a dresser of sycamores. The Lord took me from following the flock, and said to me, Go, prophecy to my people Israel. Now hear the word of the Lord" (Am 7:14–16). No wonder Amos was reluctant. Would a migrant worker who claimed to be a prophet get any better hearing today than he did?

Nor would another Jeremiah likely fare any better? He was just a teenager. The self-consciousness and clumsiness of one just emerging from adolescence will hardly be looked upon as prophetic credentials.

The word of the Lord came to me thus: Before I formed you

in the womb I knew you, before you were born I dedicated
you, a prophet to the nations I appointed you. "Ah, Lord God!"
I said, "I know not how to speak; I am too young." But the
Lord answered me, say not, "I am too young." To whom-
ever I send you, you shall go; whatever I command you, you
shall speak" (Jer 1:4-7).

The reluctance of the prophets sprang not just from
their own sense of unworthiness. They knew it was
a thankless task. They were being asked to be the
conscience of Israel, the alarm clock for a slumbering
and self-satisfied people. Such people are not especially
bright and cheery when awakened.

They have been called men sent to "comfort the
afflicted, and afflict the comfortable," no pleasant
task in any age. But those are the ages to which God
sends prophets. There are times when men smugly
say: "God's in his heaven, all's right with the world."
There. are times when personal ambitions, the prosperity of the people and national goals are confused
with God's will.

The prophets do not want to criticize, but they
must, for they are lovers. They see the possibility,
the potential of their people and they cannot remain
silent, no matter how much suffering such a thankless vocation entails.

You duped me, O Lord, and I let myself be duped; you were
too strong for me, and you triumphed. All the day I am an object of laughter; everyone mocks me. Whenever I speak, I must
cry out, violence and outrage is my message; The word of the
Lord has brought me derision and reproach all the day. I say
to myself, I will not mention him, I will speak in his name
no more. But then it becomes like fire burning in my heart,

imprisoned in my bones; I grow weary holding it in, I cannot endure it (Jer 20:7-9).

He criticizes so severely, because he loves so deeply. And when they have nothing but mockery for him, he will turn to signs to give visual expression to his message (cf. Jer. 16,19).

If the prophets harshest words are in condemnation of the "establishment," and the structures of the covenant, it is not because there is anything wrong with structure (e.g. liturgy, priesthood, authority), but because they have become ends instead of means to covenant.

This is why the prophets, although in and of the community, keep a certain distance from its structures. This allows them to retain an objectivity which gives them a clear vision. The minute they are co-opted and supported by the establishment, they are in danger of becoming false prophets. The prophet of I Kg 13, knew well that he would be compromised just by accepting the king's invitation to dinner. Independence is essential to the prophetic vocation. It is difficult to point the finger when one is being kept.

This independence can easily be misunderstood for aloofness and superiority, but that is the least of the prophet's sufferings. What grips him most deeply is that his rejection is not by enemies, but those who should know better, the very ones he loves, and to whom he has been sent. Jesus found this soon after he began his public life, as depicted in the tragic scene in the synagogue at Nazareth. "They found him too much for them." Jesus' response to all this was:

"No prophet is without honor except in his native place, among his own kindred, and in his own house" (Mk 6:4).

If there is one vocational description which would best characterize the work of Jesus it would be that of prophet. He is reluctant to be called messiah, and never claims the title of priest. He would rather be seen as the fulfillment of the promise that Moses made: "A prophet like me will the Lord your God raise up for you from among your own kinsmen; to him shall you listen" (Dt 18:15). His appearance with Moses and *the* Prophet, Elijah, at the transfiguration are an indication of the company he wished to keep. Weary of the pettiness of their leaders, the people recognized him for what he was. "They began to praise God. 'A great prophet has arisen among us,' they said; and 'God has visited his people'" (Lk 7:16).

Paul's advice to the Thessalonians (I Thes. 5:19-20) about not despising prophecies or stifling the Spirit, coupled with his insistence that the role of prophet was second only to that of apostle (I Cor 12:28), indicate how important he felt this vocation was for the Church.

Individual religious and communities today can perhaps best find their identity in this role. It is simply a return to the spirit of their own founders, prophets in their day. Religious should be people of such broad vision and openness that they can not only be prophets, but give a welcome to them. They should be the exception that proves the rule. At least some prophets are held in honor.

The vows, and the very concept of religious life, particularly of exempt communities, allow them to be at the service of the Church they love, and yet somewhat independent of its structure. With great vision and mobility they should be able to move ahead, perceiving where the needs of God's people may be calling them, and constantly renewing themselves as a sign for the whole Church. In a life lived totally in covenant they can still call out with the voice of their founders if they will welcome the prophetic dimension of their call.

19.

RESTORING
_____ALL THINGS IN CHRIST

Times of crisis and desperation may lead the ordinary person to alienation and hopelessness. For the man and woman of faith, they can lead to deeper union with God and a broader perception of the vision that only faith can give.

The hopeless situation of the exile gave birth to both the creation account of Genesis I, and the magnificent meditation on creation and redemption of Isaiah 40ff. These men of faith, desperately in need of salvation, looked to the wonders of creation about them, and knew from the very fact that they could touch his handiwork, 'so could they touch the saving hand of their God.

Do you not know or have you not heard? The Lord is the eternal God, creator of the ends of the earth. He does not faint nor grow weary, and his knowledge is beyond scrutiny. He gives strength to the fainting; for the weak he makes vigor abound. Though young men faint and grow weary, and youths stagger and fall, they that hope in the Lord will renew their strength (Is 40:28–31a).

For some, the exile was just a time of chaos, time that lay heavy on their hands. For others, it was a time of new creation, of deeper understanding of the role of Yahweh, not just in a little patch of land called

Judea, but in the entire universe.

In the New Testament, we find a similar situation. Paul, in a sense is in exile, for he is in prison. The letters he writes from there, Ephesians and Colossians, are thus called captivity epistles. They show the mature reflection of Paul on the meaning of the Christ event. Isolated from the community, he could have spent the time feeling sorry for himself. Instead he reflects and theologizes on the person of Christ. Like Israel he had personally experienced the saving action of the Lord. Now he asks himself about the role of Jesus, not only in salvation but in all of creation.

The question is brought into focus for Paul by problems that have arisen in the churches. Like the Galatians who would not be satisfied that the Good News was Jesus, period, and not Jesus and the law, these Christians wanted a religion of Jesus and . . . ! They were the kind of people who would not leave the house in the morning, without checking their horoscopes, lest they be advised to go back to bed. They had not yet emerged from their pagan beliefs in the existence of all manner of superterrestial forces, each charged with some area of life and creation, intermediaries between God and man. Each of these powers, thrones, or principalities, however they might be called, must be understood and propitiated if life was not to be a constant chaos.

They had a system that made sense out of life, and made it livable. As Christians they wanted to know where Christ fit into that system. They recognized him as another intermediary between God and man, but were uncertain as to his function in relation to the other intermediaries.

Enter Paul. Jesus doesn't fit into the system, he is the system. He isn't part of the plan of God, he is the plan of God. He doesn't control one area of life; life itself does not make sense without him. He doesn't exercise power over one portion of the universe, he is its very heart beat and center of gravity.

"Through him we have the forgiveness of our sins" (Col 1:14), but that by no means exhausts his role in the Father's plan.

He is the image of the invisible God, the first-born of all creatures. In him everything in heaven and on earth was created, things visible and invisible, whether thrones or dominations, principalities or powers; all were created through him, and for him. He is before all else that is. In him everything continues in being. It is he who is the head of the body, the church; he who is the beginning, the first-born of the dead, so that primacy may be his in everything. It pleased God to make absolute fullness reside in him and, by means of him, to reconcile everything in his person, both on earth and in the heavens, making peace through the blood of his cross (Col 1:15-20).

In addition to other words that imply totality and fulness, no less than seven times in this short passage does Paul shout out "all," "everything." Without denying the existence of their "things invisible" he insists that, if they exist, they have no other meaning except in, through and for Jesus Christ. There is no angel, man, animal, flower or particle of creation that has any reason for existence except in him. If the mountains, seas, and rivers; sun, moon and stars; animal, bird and insect could sing out, they would form a chorus proclaiming that they were made for the sake of the Word Incarnate.

This vision, as rich and deep as it is, and coming as it does as the fruit of Paul's mature reflection on the mystery of Christ, is almost more than our minds can grasp. Like him, we are used to thinking of events chronologically. It can be a dizzying experience as we go with Paul, penetrating the timeless, eternal, plan of God, "his word in all its fullness, that mystery hidden from ages and generations past, but now revealed to his holy ones."

.Like a drowning man who does not ask the credentials of his rescuer, Paul had experienced the saving grace of Jesus. Now that he has his feet on dry land he finds out about his Savior, and his role, not only in relation to Paul and all mankind, but the entire universe.

Paul sees that Jesus comes among men not as an alien, for they were made for him. He comes to this world, not as a stranger, for it is his home; it was made for him.

Because of the chronology in which the Bible was written, and our own consciousness of time, we tend to think of creation, Adam, fall, and then of Jesus Christ, almost as an afterthought in the mind of God. Not so, says Paul. In the eternity of God's plan even we have a priority over creation, although chronologically we came much later.

Praised be the God and the Father of our Lord Jesus Christ who has bestowed on us in Christ every spiritual blessing in .the heavens! God chose us in him before the world began, to

be holy and blameless in his sight, to be full of love; he likewise predestined us through Christ Jesus to be his adopted
sons—such was his will and pleasure—that all might praise
the glorious favor he has bestowed on us in his beloved. It
is in Christ and through his blood that we have been re-
deemed and our sins forgiven, so immeasurably generous is
God's favor to us. God has given us the wisdom to understand
fully the mystery, the plan he was pleased to decree in Christ,
to be carried out in the fullness of time: namely, to bring all
things in the heavens and on earth into one under Christ's
headship (Eph 1:3-10).

Before the world was made, we were already in
God's plan, to be his sons, the brothers and sisters
of Jesus Christ, in whom we were chosen, predestined and adopted. This is because Jesus was no afterthought in the plan of God. He is the plan of God.
Even Adam and all who came after him until the
fullness of time, had no other reason for existence
except in Jesus. Incarnation was not a stop-gap effort.
It was the very reason for creation. Tertullian's cry,
"O anima naturaliter Christiana," "O Soul, that is by
its very nature Christian," hits the mark. The same
can be said of the universe. By its very nature it is
Christian, for it is in, through and for him. Because
of God's eternal plan for the Incarnation, there has
always been a sacramental quality to creation, perceived by such men who were totally wrapped in
Christ as Francis of Assisi.

Another Francis, de Sales, the gentle saint of Geneva
has a beautiful meditation on this vision of Paul's in
his "Treatise on the Love of God." He recognizes our
difficulty in grasping it, and says it should be compared to a man who desires some wine. That is first

in his mind, but will come last, after the planting of the vineyard, harvesting of the grapes and fermentation of the juice. Like Christ in the fullness of time, the wine is first in priority of intention, yet last to come into existence.

Thus for Paul, redemption determines the way that Christ came, not the fact that he came. Adam did not effect his coming, but the manner in which he came. And he comes to a world, that though made for him, does not recognize him. It is a world that the converts of Paul had been accused of turning upside down (such is the Greek of Acts 17:6). They knew better. In restoring it to Christ, they were turning it right side up.

This is what Paul means when he speaks of what is to be accomplished in the fullness of time "to bring all things in the heavens and on the earth into one under Christ's headship" (Eph 1:10). This is the work of restoring all things in Christ. It is putting them back where they belong, bringing all things to a head, which is Jesus Christ himself.

The Church is to be the sign of that unity in him, that was intended in eternity for the entire universe. "He has put all things under Christ's feet, and has made him, thus exalted, the head of the church, which is his body: the fullness of him who fills the universe in all its parts" (Eph 1:22,23).

The Eucharist, the sign and source of the Church's activity, speaks of this plan of God. Matter, being transformed into a meaning that is Christ; that is, the Eucharist. In a different, but very real way, will the entire universe be transformed. It must be restored to a meaning which is totally found in Christ.

Is there an apostolate, an area of activity that is alien to religious, whose goal can be no less than Paul's vision, the Father's plan? Hardly. Wherever our lives touch with his love there is apostolate. Whereever we have moved one step to transform the universe, to tell men why they exist, then we are bringing to reality the words he taught us: "Thy kingdom come, thy will be done."

20.

_____FAITHFUL TO THE VISION

In primitive societies witch doctors and priests were entrusted with taking the chaotic and disturbing elements out of life. Their role was to control the mysterious forces that could create problems if they were not placated. But this function was really a negative one. It just made life liveable. In order that life might be more than that, there arose men known as shamans. The role of the shaman was to grasp the mystery, adventure and vision of life and share it with the community. His was almost a contemplative function, dealing not with the problems of life but with life itself. The community encouraged and supported him for he had a wisdom, a vision, which he shared with them. Without him they were in danger of getting lost in their own affairs and preoccupations. He showed them that there was more to life than that.

The Bible may be said to have been written by inspired shamans, men who were able to capture the vision of covenant life with God, and share it. It is also a book about shamans. We would never have known thē vision of faith if Abraham had not first plunged into its mystery and shared it with others. We would not have known of the reality and possibility of the Paschal mystery if Moses had not perceived that life can be more than slavery, and shared his vision of Yahweh and his gracious invitation with the people of the first passover.

But life has a tendency to get us bogged down. There's always the tendency to be preoccupied with our own cares, and become introspective and cynical. We need someone to open our eyes, to awaken in us the depth and breadth of vision without which life is just a dreary plodding along. This loss of enthusiasm can literally be a deadening process. Slowly but surely, not with a decisive "I will not serve," but with a creeping paralysis, man is alienated from God, and it shows in his lifestyle. Israel did not raise a clenched fist and say "no" to God. It was a long drawn out process of the vision becoming ever dimmer.

The book of Deuteronomy was written in just such times of mediocrity and lukewarmness. Written by unknown author(s), it was composed in the eighth or seventh century before Christ about five hundred years after the death of Moses. The author(s) present it as if it were a series of homilies given by Moses to God's people, on the verge of entering into the promised land. In reality it is an attempt to recall a later generation to their first fervor. Jeremiah, who used the book (*cf.* Jer 11) in his own efforts toward *aggiornamento,* sums up it spirit and vision in his preaching in the sixth century.

This word of the Lord came to me: Go, cry out this message for Jerusalem to hear! I remember the devotion of your youth, how you loved me as a bride, following me in the desert, in a land unsown. Does a virgin forget her jewelry, a bride her sash? Yet my people have forgotten me days without number

(Jer 2:1,2, and 32).

The message of Deuteronomy can be summed up in three words: remember, today, and love. It is an attempt to get the people to remember what God has done, to get them to recall the vision he once gave them. If they can grasp that, then it will evoke an immediate response today, and they will share his love in community. For many reasons the attempted renewal by Deuteronomy failed in its day. Its success can only be seen later when it becomes the most frequently quoted book in the New Testament. Jesus and the primitive community both grasped the timelessness of its message. They knew that every day they must renew the vision, otherwise they would cease to be a community of love.

It is just such a vision that John presents Jesus sharing with his disciples the night before he died. His last discourse on love and the Holy Spirit who will keep it alive in them is a marvelous sharing of his vision when he could have been preoccupied with his own impending death. He knew that if they were not to share the fate of Israel they must be a people of vibrant vision, ever renewed.

How desperately they needed that was shown by their own fear and self pity as they gathered after his death (Jn 20:19ff.). After his Resurrection, his appearance among them was not only a reality, but it was a vision that they were to keep alive and share. It was the Spirit who gave them the power to do so. With that vision they ceased being concerned about their own welfare and proclaimed that they themselves

were the ones of whom Joel prophesied. Their enthusiasm was not from drunkenness, but from the
overwhelming reality of their vision.

Peter stood up with the Eleven, raised his voice, and addressed
them: "You who are Jews, indeed all of you staying in Jerusalem! Listen to what I have to say. You must realize that
these men are not drunk, as you seem to think. It is only nine
in the morning! No, it is what Joel the prophet spoke of: It
shall come to pass in the last days, says God, that I will pour
out a portion of my spirit on all mankind: Your sons and
daughters shall prophesy, your young men shall see visions and
your old men shall dream dreams (Acts 2:14–17).

They had a vision of Jesus Christ, risen, alive, and
real. St. Augustine once wrote that dispersed among
the wisdom of the sages and religious men of the past
can be found everything that is in the Gospels, except
one verse. "The Word was made flesh and made his
dwelling among us" (Jn 1:14). That is the vision, that
is what the Apostles had to share. Instead of sitting
around holding hands and lamenting their fate, saying woe is us, they enthusiastically shared their vision.
"Some three thousand were added that day" (Acts
2:41).

Lest, with a romantic sense of the past, we think
that we would have been enthusiastic if we had been
there, too, we should not just dwell on Pentecost,
but go on to the epistles. Their very existence is an
indication that the early Church had to struggle to
keep the vision alive and vibrant just as much as we
do. Most of Paul's letters were written to solve problems in communities where the vision had become

obscured and confused. More than problem solving, however, they are a sharing of "that mystery hidden from ages and generations past, but now revealed to his holy ones . . . the mystery of Christ in you, your hope of glory " (Col 2:26,27). He asks that the Philippians (2:2ff.) "make my joy complete by your unanimity, possessing the one love, united in spirit and ideals." He then shares with them the magnificent poem which is his own vision of Christ.

Paul has a favorite word that he uses for the mature Christian. It comes from the Greek *telos,* meaning end, goal or purpose. He uses *teleioi* to describe those who are no longer immature, acting like children, simply interested in whatever little thing engages their attention at the present moment. They will act maturely, because they have a goal, purpose and vision. They are mature, not because they have arrived, but because they know where they are going.

It is he who gave apostles, prophets, evangelists, pastors and teachers in roles of service for the faithful to build up the body of Christ, till we become one in faith and the knowledge of God's Son, and form that perfect man who is Christ come to full stature. Let us, then, be children no longer, tossed here and there, carried about by every wind of doctrine that originates in human trickery and skill in proposing error. Rather, let us profess the truth in love and grow to the full maturity of Christ the head. Through him the whole body grows, and with the proper functioning of the members joined firmly together by each supporting ligament, builds itself up in love (Eph 4:11–16).

Paul knew that a community, no matter how they differed on the means, would not be polarized if they actively and with love, shared the same end or vision. That would be the sign of their maturity. Without that they would be children, united or divided only by the games they played.

The letter to the Hebrews is a magnificent example of sharing the vision. It was written for those who were discouraged and in danger of throwing up their hands and saying, "it's not worth it." Life in the Church, in the community, was not meeting their expectations, and was growing tedious. The author puts his finger on the problem: their vision was obscured. They started yearning after the "good old days" when life was organized by the law, and the countless sacrifices of the temple made them feel religious.

He starts out by telling them how partial and fragmentary was the vision to which they want to return, compared to what they have in Jesus Christ (Heb 1:1–4). He sees that they have arrived at their present state of despondency because they have not shared their vision, encouraging each other (Heb 3:12). Several times he advises them "Fix your eyes on Jesus" (3:1). This is the same Jesus who knows what they are going through "Let us hold fast to our profession of faith. For we do not have a high priest who is unable to sympathize with our weakness, but one who was tempted in every way that we are, yet never sinned" (4:14,15).

He must have had a vision of our day, for he sees a community that is sick and tired of meetings. But he knows of no other way, as burdensome as it may be.

Let us hold unswervingly to our profession which gives us hope, for he who made the promise deserves our trust. We must consider how to rouse each other to love and good deeds. We should not absent ourselves from the assembly, as some do, but encourage one another (Heb 10:23-25a).

His words could have been written, not 2,000 years ago, but after yesterday's community meeting. "Strengthen your drooping hands, and your weak knees. Make straight the paths you walk on, that your halting limbs may not be dislocated, but healed" (12:12,13).

His concluding words could have been written directly for us who are trying to return to the spirit of our founders.

Remember your leaders who spoke the word of God to you; consider how their lives ended, and imitate their faith. Jesus Christ is the same yesterday, today, and forever (Heb 13:7,8).

We can never recapture the charism of our founders. God has given us our own. But we can recapture that which made their gifts so effective in the service of the Church, their vision. If we are discouraged, and worried about a crisis in religious life, maybe our failure to encourage each other and share our vision is the reason. Peter shared his vision and got three thousand converts. Perhaps our lack of vocations is the result of being so polarized over inconsequentials that we have allowed our vision to be obscured.

May he enlighten your innermost vision that you may know the great hope to which he has called you, the wealth of his glorious heritage to be distributed among the members of the church, and the immeasurable scope of his power in us who believe (Eph 1:18).

21.

SUFFERING SERVANTS

A man's confrontation with the problem of evil will determine his view of all of life and reality. When it is a question of moral evil he may not be terribly mystified. Men are responsible, and good men are the proof that life need not be a chaotic morass in the control of evil men. Even at Dachau, as horrible as it was, men could say that it need not have been so. Men are responsible.

It is when the confrontation is with the stench of death from an earthquake in Peru, with the distended stomachs of children in drought ridden Africa, with the pitiful cries of a dying child, or with the cancer gnawing away at my own life that we grasp for reasons. Why? Why should life be like this? How can life be like this if it is true that the God who calls is good, kind and loving? Where is he when the order and harmony of creation are clouded over by the chaos of evil and suffering?

The Persians, seeing that light and darkness, night and day, seem to be at a tug of war in the universe, concluded that all of life and reality were involved in the contest. It was presided over by the god of light and goodness and the god of darkness and evil. The material world was the realm of the god of darkness and the spiritual, the realm of the god of light, who would eventually triumph. Man just had to wait. In his early years, St. Augustine was a believer in this Manicheism which despised the flesh and the world as being what prevented man from being truly spiritual. If such an intellect could believe in it, it has to be an engaging philosophy. But he also learned that it is totally alien to the Gospel.

In our own times the existentialist philosophers found a different solution to the tension between belief in a good God and the very real presence of chaotic evil and suffering in their experience. They simply accepted the chaos as proof that faith makes no sense. There is no God. They look upon belief in a God of love as no more of a solution than Manicheism was. There is no God of love. There is no orderly creation, except that which man brings about. Life has no meaning except that which I put into it. It is when man realistically accepts the meaninglessness of life that he can begin to do something about it.

A Christian might find this a presumptuous and unpalatable alternative to belief in God, but at least it does make us aware that our simple answers attributing all to the "Will of God" may not be any closer to the mark than atheism.

As they did with the evil of poverty, the early Biblical theologians, the Deuteronomists, solved the problem of evil and suffering by making God responsible. Suffering is his way of getting back at unfaithful man. Thus, the only thing to do is to stay on his good side and then you won't have to worry about suffering, for it will not touch your life (cf. Dt 28).

But Psalm 73 is evidence that life just did not work

out that way. Sometimes it looked like the Lord did not know whose side he was on, and this can lead to a crisis of faith.

How good God is to the upright; the Lord, to those who are clean of heart! But, as for me, I almost lost my balance; my feet all but slipped, because I was envious of the arrogant when I saw them prosper though they were wicked. Is it but in vain I have ke)t my heart clean and washed my hands as an innocent man? For I suffer affliction day after day and chastisement with each new dawn (Ps 73:1–3; 13,14).

But this momentary reverie about whether the old theology really corresponds to experience is clouded over. The prosperity and health of the wicked is only a temporary condition. God will eventually get them.

How suddenly they are made desolate! They are completely wasted away amid horrors. As though they were the dream of one who had awakened, O Lord, so will you, when you arise, set at nought these phantoms (Ps 73:19,20).

The author of this Psalm, however, comes to the realization that, if the evil and suffering of life cause a problem in belief, life makes no sense whatsoever without God.

Whom else have I in heaven? And when I am with you, the earth delights me not. Though my flesh and my heart waste away, God is the rock of my heart and my portion forever (Ps 73:25,26).

In this and many other Psalms the problem of evil and suffering is not solved, but a step is made in the right direction: it is put in perspective. God is the overpowering reality in a universe in which evil and suffering are but a part. To use Chesterton's analogy, throwing up ones hands in disbelief when confronted with suffering is like throwing out a beautiful stained glass window because one small piece is broken.

Job is the classic old testament figure who is caught in the dilemma. Although a later author added a preface and conclusion that reverted to the simple solution of prosperity as a reward, and vice versa, the core of the book shows that such an approach just does not work. In spite of the protestations of his wife and friends, Job is conscious of no guilt that should have caused such sufferings. In desperation he cries out for a defense lawyer.

Oh, that I had one to hear my case, and that my accuser would write out his indictment! Surely, I should wear it on my shoulder or put it on me like a diadem; of all my steps I should give him an account; like a prince I should present myself before him. This is my final plea; let the Almighty answer me (Job 31:35-37)!

Much to his surprise, God answers him, but not with the answer he wants.

Who is this that obscures divine plans with words of ignorance? Gird up your loins now, like a man; I will question you, and you tell me the answers! Where were you when I founded the earth? Tell me, if you have understanding (Job 38:2-4).

There is no question, that according to the old the-

ology Job was not guilty. But in view of the total
mystery of God, his creation, and his holiness, should
Job not at least stand back and say those most difficult words, "I do not know?" Does God have to reveal
every little thing, so that life can be computerized?
Job does stand back, and for the first time, suffering
is seen not as a problem to be solved, but a mystery
in which one can deepen one's faith.

I have dealt with great things that I do not understand;
things too wonderful for me, which I cannot know. I had heard
of you by word of mouth, but now my eye has seen you, therefore I disown what I have said, and repent in dust and ashes
(Job 42:3-6).

Even years before the story of Job, the mystery of
suffering was penetrated by the "suffering servant."
In him it is perceived not just as something to be
tolerated in a chaotic world. The Servant shows the
good, the wholeness, the peace, the *shalom* that can
come to other men when one man suffers with love
and obedience.

Yet it was our infirmities that he bore, our sufferings that he
endured, while we thought of him as stricken, as one smitten
by God and afflicted. But he was pierced for our offenses,
crushed for our sins; upon him was the chastisement that makes
us whole, by his stripes we were healed (Is 53:4,5).

Here is a revelation, as startling for its insight as it
is for the way it was so quickly forgotten.
The story of the man born blind (Jn 9) shows that
even the disciples of Jesus could think of no other
way to explain evil and suffering except in terms of

God's getting even. And as the Old Testament did not, Jesus does not solve the problem of suffering. He brushes away the simple solution of Deuteronomic theology, but gives no other. "Rather, it was to let God's works show forth in him." It is no solution to suffering, but it does show that God can use even that to manifest himself, and to bring forth faith.

While Jesus teaches that the good God will not be forever patient in tolerating men's evil deeds, but will punish them (Mt 23:35), it is evident that he does not lump all suffering in this category. Because no disciple is greater than his master (Mt 10:24), his followers can expect to suffer as he does, and that can hardly be at the hands of a God who is getting even!

Jesus' own suffering and death on the cross, the pattern for every disciple (Mt 16:24) can be considered nothing less than the horrible evil they were. But with love and obedience he showed how they could be transformed. The Father was not a bloodthirsty ogre who sought the death of his Son. That was but the means by which Jesus showed his total obedience and love.

From that day to this, his love and obedience in the face of suffering and death, have had their effect over space and time. What men considered tragic and evil, Jesus grasped with obedience and love, and at this moment you and I are experiencing the result. Because of it, to the glory of God the Father, we can proclaim: "Jesus Christ is Lord" (cr. Phil 2:6–11).

However, since he did not, neither can we limit his sufferings to the last three days of Holy Week. With love, he took on all the sufferings of the human condition (Heb 2:14ff.). He was no stranger to hunger, thirst, temptation, fatigue, misunderstanding from the pettiness of those he loved and all the other sufferings that are part of being human. But he transformed them in love and obedience.

While the role of the disciple is to alleviate the evils of suffering as Jesus did (Mt 16:30), it is also the disciple's task to continue his redemptive work of suffering in love and obedience. Even from his prison cell, unable to go forth and preach the Gospel, Paul knew what he could do.

Even now I find my joy in the suffering I endure for you. In my own flesh I fill up what is lacking in the sufferings of Christ for the sake of his body, the church (Col 1:24).

Jesus never solved the problem of suffering, but he did show that a Christian far from being overwhelmed and broken, can use suffering in the mystery of love. Catastrophes which insurance companies still call "acts of God" may leave us wondering. But a Christian need not wonder about what to do with the suffering around him and within him. He continues the work of Christ.

In an age where activity too often becomes the measure of productivity, it is well to remember that those in hospitals, infirmaries and retirement homes may be accomplishing more for the Kingdom than those who teach, preach and write books. Far from being burdens on a community, their suffering with love may make the activities of all the other members of the community possible. If days in bed seem useless, so did three hours on a cross!

22.

THE SPIRIT
IN THE COMMUNITY

Times of renewal and reformation invariably disturb and unsettle communities. The border between *aggiornamento* and chaos is not always well posted. "Who's in charge here?" "Whatever happened to the good old days, when we knew where we were going?" Such sighs for a return to stability are but echoes in our day from all the renewals and times of reform in the past. The Hebrews wanted to go back to Egypt. Some of the early Christians wanted to go back to the law.

The yearning for authority, a guide who will lead, a map, a groundplan, is typical of such times. This is precisely why the Israelites saw the law as such a great gift of God. It left no room for guesswork. The law was the very personification of wisdom, and the proof of the greatness of God.

Such is our God; no other is to be compared to him: He has traced out all the way of understanding, and has given her to Jacob, his servant, to Israel, his beloved son. Since then she has appeared on earth, and moved among men. She is the book of the precepts of God, the law that endures forever; all who cling to her will live, but those will die who forsake her. Turn, O Jacob, and receive her: walk by her light toward splendor. Give not your glory to another, your privileges to an alien race. Blessed are we, O Israel; for what pleases God is known to us (Bar 3:36-4:4)!

This glory, privilege, and spelling out of the will of God was what so many of the early Christian were reluctant to be left without. They found the message of Jesus to be much less detailed than they had been accustomed to. It was one thing to be told that they were the light of the world and salt of the earth, and that they were to follow the great commandment of love, but practically, how were they to live this out?

Before Jesus had ascended, it had been no problem. They could ask him. But now they felt lost and wanted to get back to a set pattern of life. As yet, they saw no substitute for the law.

After the Ascension, however, John reminds them that there is a substitute for Jesus. Recalling the words of Jesus at the last supper, he instructs them that there is one among them who has the exact same function in their midst as Jesus had. In a sense, he is a surrogate Jesus.

I will ask the Father and he will give you another Paraclete— to be with you always: the Spirit of truth, whom the world cannot accept, since it neither sees him nor recognizes him; but you can recognize him because he remains with you and will be within you. The Paraclete, the Holy Spirit whom the Father will send in my name, will instruct you in everything, and remind you of all that I told you (Jn 14:16, 17, 26).

Judging from the many children who call him the parakeet, the title given by Jesus to the Holy Spirit is not a familiar one to us. The other translation, advocate, does let us know that it is a term for defense lawyer, advisor, guide in times of difficulty. What Jesus had been for his disciples while he was

on earth, the Holy Spirit is to be in the post-pente-
cost community. To look for something other than the
Spirit as a guide is to look for something other than
Jesus. He knew what he was doing, and he provided
neither constitution nor code of law. He handed over
the Spirit.

But, while the Gospels tell us how Jesus functioned
in the community, how does the Holy Spirit function?
In a previous chapter of John, Jesus has already warned
us to be ready for surprises, for the work of the Spirit
is like the wind, which blows where it wills (3:8).
Getting hold of him is like getting hold of an armful
of wind!

In this final discourse to his disciples, when Jesus
tells them he will not leave them orphans, he also
tells them some of the things that the Spirit will accomplish among them. He will be for them the "Spirit
of truth" (14:17). This reference is not to speculative
truth or a body of truths. He will be for them the
Spirit of truth because he is the Spirit of Jesus, the
way, the truth, and the life (14:6). Here is meant Biblical "truth" whose absence Hosea so bitterly lamented
in the Israelites who no longer walked in covenant
Thus, the Spirit will enable the believer to lead the
true, the real life instead of the sham life which the
"world" offers.

Earlier (I Cor 12:3) Paul had spoken of this role of
the Spirit. "No one can say 'Jesus is Lord,' except in
the Holy Spirit." The power to acknowledge the Lordship of Jesus in the life of the individual and community is a sign of the presence of the Spirit. He
enables us to be stripped of anything else that con-

trols our lives except Jesus Christ. The more truthfully I can say "Jesus is Lord," of my life, my activity, my goals, the more certain I can be of the presence of the Spirit. He helps us sweep away whatever is not Jesus.

Paul frequently contrasts the man of the Spirit with the man of the flesh, in order to bring the work of the Spirit more sharply into focus.

There is no condemnation now for those who are in Christ Jesus. The law of the spirit, the spirit of life in Christ Jesus, has freed you from the law of sin and death. The law was powerless because of its weakening by the flesh. Then God sent his son in the likeness of sinful flesh as a sin offering, thereby condemning sin in the flesh, so that the just demands of the law might be fulfilled in us who live, not according to the flesh, but according to the spirit. Those who live according to the flesh are intent on the things of the flesh, those who live according to the spirit, on those of the spirit. The tendency of the flesh is toward death but that of the spirit toward life and peace. The flesh in its tendency is at enmity with God; it is not subject to God's law. Indeed, it cannot be; those who are in the flesh cannot please God. But you are not in the flesh; you are in the spirit, since the Spirit of God dwells in you. If anyone does not have the Spirit of Christ, he does not belong to Christ. If Christ is in you, the body is dead because of sin, while the spirit lives because of justice. If the Spirit of him who raised Jesus from the dead dwells in you, then he who raised Christ from the dead will bring your mortal bodies to life also, through his Spirit dwelling in you (Rom 8:1-11).

The flesh is man's intrinsic weakness, impotency and alienation from God. The Spirit transforms into the spiritual, having strength, power, and life with God.

Paul's main problem with the law, associated with sin and death (8:2,3) was that it could only point the way. It was powerless to help us get there.

On the contrary, the Spirit both points the way, and enables us to get there, for it is the very Spirit of him who raised Jesus from the dead, dwelling in us. The Spirit empowers us to live the true, the authentic existence because he leads us ever more deeply into the mystery of the Lordship of Jesus, and away from all that is not Jesus: law, sin, and death.

But we are not yet in heaven. The flesh of selfishness and death is too much with us. There is a tug-of-war within us (Rom 7:13ff.). We are like the universe about us which is in the throes of labor pains, until it have no other meaning except in Jesus Christ (Col 1:20). "Yes, we know that all creation groans and is in agony, even until now. Not only that, but we ourselves, although we have the Spirit as first fruits, groan inwardly while we await the redemption of our bodies" (Rom 8:22,23).

It is in this time of growth that the Spirit does his work. "The Paraclete, the Holy Spirit, whom the Father will send in my name, will instruct you in everything, and remind you of all that I told you." (Jn 14:26). Jesus does not promise that the Spirit will write a book, draw a map or provide a code of law. Since he is the substitute for Jesus, he does what Jesus did. But what Jesus did and said was ignored, except by those who were aware of who he was. They gave themselves to him in discipleship, went apart with him and listened to him. The same must be true of those who live in the Spirit.

The presence of the Spirit may be less tangible, but it is no less real than was the presence of Jesus to his disciples. The Spirit's voice may be less audible, but Jesus promised it would be there—for those who would listen.

In John 16:7ff. Jesus speaks of a threefold conviction that the Spirit will lay upon the "world." (In John's vocabulary, "world" is not material creation, but is similar to Paul's "flesh": all that is not Jesus and opposes him.) In these condemnations, the Spirit also speaks to Christians, for in them he points out what is not of Jesus.

"He will prove the world wrong . . . about sin, in that they refuse to believe in me." Sin in the Bible is missing the mark, missing the goal, going one's own merry way. The Jews thought it was breaking the law. The Spirit tells us that it is lack of faith in Jesus. Thus the Christian and the community are given the first criterion for decision making. Will it lead to Jesus, and build up faith in him? Decisions were easy before. One only had to ask if an action was legal. Now, all things must be weighed in the light of Jesus and his Kingdom if we are not to fall under the Spirit's condemnation.

"He will prove the world wrong . . . about justice, from the fact that I go to the Father and you can see me no more." The authorities thought justice had been done in putting Jesus to death, in the name of God and religion! The real justice was accomplished in his Resurrection and Ascension. The Spirit thus gives a second criterion for Christian activity. As religious as we may think ourselves, and as solidly rooted in the will of God as we'd like to consider ourselves, we must always be prepared to be proven wrong, and be ready to change. The condemnation of Jesus came about through the leaders of organized religion who were too organized. Their will had to be God's. Their voices cried out so loud they could not hear the voice of God. Thus a Christian must always be ready to continue searching for God's will, for fear that he might have confused it with his own.

"He will prove the world wrong . . . about condemnation, for the prince of this world has been condemned." Jesus continues to turn the tables. They were too ready to condemn the wrong one. Later on, their own great Rabbi Gamaliel asks them not to make the same mistake in condemning the Christian community; "Let them alone. If their purpose or activity is human in origins, it will destroy itself. If on the other hand, it comes from God, you will not be able to destroy them without fighting God himself" (Acts 5:38). In an age when the Prince of this World has been condemned, the Spirit sometimes asks that we have patience. Discerning if he is at work in an event or activity takes time.

And when all this has been said, we still find him blowing like the wind. So did the primitive community at Pentecost (Acts 2:2). He is Jesus' gift to us, no less than he was to them. The difference is that they stopped sitting around lamenting the good old days of law and order. They realized they were not orphans. Their awareness of the Spirit gave them an enthusiasm that was contagious. They were willing to live in the Spirit and let him pray in them (Rom 8:26).

23.

WAITING FOR THE LORD

Two tendencies arise in the Old Testament, both of which are a caricature of its legitimate theology. The first springs from the fact that God, who liberated his people from oppression in the past will do so again in the future. The more difficult were the times in which they lived, the more fervently did they look forward to the Day of the Lord. This is a legitimate aspiration, asking the creator to touch and breathe once again upon the present chaos. When grounded in covenant faith it shows a hope and expectancy which Jesus later put into words. "Thy kingdom come, thy will be done."

In Israel, however, it came to be identified with the nationalistic desire for Yahweh to intervene against those who were causing the chaos and oppression, their enemies. (Who must also be his enemies, they thought.) Amos informs them that they are the enemies, and the Day of the Lord will be darkness and not light for them (5:18). They looked forward to a day when they would have no worries or cares, tension would cease and all their needs would be taken care of. But they forgot that their basic need was for God.

The second tendency arose from Yahweh's call for a strong faith, even when the present situation looks impossible and one must hope against hope as Abraham did (Rom 4:13). But if faith tells me that God is on my side, then what's wrong with taking the present tension and difficult situation into my own hands and resolving it according to my plan, which after all must be his?

What's wrong is that my plan may not be his, and having faith in him may well involve living with the tension and imperfection, and letting him do the weeding in his own time (Mt 13:24ff.).

The incident that resulted in the Emmanuel prophecy is a classic example of this tendency (Is 7). Jerusalem was about to be destroyed by her enemies who wanted to put a non-Davidic king on the throne, thus nullifying the messianic promise (2 Sam 7:16). King Ahaz could not bear the tension. "The heart of the king and the heart of the people trembled as the trees of the forest tremble in the wind" (Is 7:2). The king decided to take matters into his own hands. Yahweh did not seem to be moving fast enough, so Ahaz sacrificed his son, the Davidic heir, to the Assyrian god (2 Kg 16:3) and then made a covenant with the Assyrian King (2 Kg 16:7ff.). He was inspecting the water supply, leaving nothing to chance (or to Yahweh) when Isaiah met him (7:4). No wonder he feigned piety and would not ask a sign from the Lord; he had already taken care of everything himself.

Nevertheless, the Lord gives a sign. A baby, not an army, a child, not military power is the sign that God is with us, Emmanuel. The Davidic promise, one day to be fulfilled in another child, "God with us," is not broken.

The presumption and despair manifested by these two tendencies when confronted with crisis and tension point out the dilemma that life in covenant involves. One looks forward to pie in the sky, by and by and calls for the God who is the "fac totum" and "cure all" to get a move on. The other, equally unsettled by the present tension takes matters into its own hands, leaving God out of the picture.

The new testament witnesses that the Christian must steer clear of both hazards. He has his eyes on the future and he yearns for the fulness of the Kingdom, and the perfect community in Christ.

I heard a loud voice from the throne cry out: "This is God's dwelling among men. He shall dwell with them and they shall be his people and he shall be their God who is always with them. He shall wipe every tear from their eyes, and there shall be no more death or mourning, crying out or pain, for the former world has passed away." The One who sat on the throne said to me, "See, I make all things new!" The One who gives this testimony says, "Yes, I am coming soon!" Amen! Come, Lord Jesus! (Rev 21:3-5a; 22:20)

At the same time, he has his feet on the ground, where there is tension, growth and imperfection. As a disciple he knows that his role, like Jesus' own, is to relieve tension where possible, encourage growth to maturity and to strive for perfection, "on earth as it is in heaven." He may never sit back and throw his hands up. Neither may he, however be unrealistic. Tension, growth and imperfection are part of the human condition which Jesus took upon himself, and did not release his followers from (Heb 2:17; 4:15;

5:7ff.).

The convert, the novice, as well as the apostle want everything perfect at once. The apostles did not want to take the time for prayer and fasting that some devils require to be cast out. They did not want to tolerate those who were inhospitable to Jesus and wanted to destroy the Samaritan towns. Jesus had to remind them that the Kingdom is like leaven that needs time, like a seed that cannot be rushed to growth, and like a field in which both grain and weeds grow until the harvest.

The apostles were typical of us all. In their precipitous haste to bring about the perfect kingdom, they found a coverup for their own imperfection. Can the patience of God be more clearly manifested than in what Jesus had to put up with while encouraging them to growth and maturity? Look what happened to Peter after his vociferous protestations of loyalty. And Jesus still did not give up on him. But he did warn them all of the subterfuge of the perfectionist who is very strict . . . with others!

Why look at the speck in your brother's eye when you miss the plank in your own? How can you say to your brother, 'Let me take that speck out of your eye,' while all the time the plank remains in your own? You hypocrite! Remove the plank from your own eye first; then you will see clearly to take the speck from your brother's eye (Mt 7:3-5).

Time and again Paul calls the Christians to perfection and maturity. But he would never have had to write any of his letters if it had happened over night. Even with his own native impetuosity he was willing to admit that he had not arrived (Phil 3:12). He recognized that Christian growth involves bearing one another's burdens and thus fulfilling the law of Christ (Gal 6:2). He finally recognized what a false sense of perfection the law had given him (Gal 3:4) and refused to allow such an appearance of perfection to substitute for the slow, painful process of growth in Christ. "Love is patient" is not a theory he learned in a book.

At the same time, he never loses sight of the goal. In the letter to the Philippians he goes right to the heart of the dilemma that creates the inherent tension in Christian life.

> For, to me, "life" means Christ; hence dying is so much gain. If, on the other hand, I am to go on living in the flesh, that means productive toil for me—and I do not know which to prefer. I am strongly attracted by both: I long to be freed from this life and to be with Christ, for that is the far better thing (Phil 1:21-23).

This enthusiasm for the fulness of life in Christ, for the *parousia,* was so contagious in the early Church, that Paul and the communities he evangelized thought that it was right around the corner. It is the main topic of the first letters that he wrote, the epistles to the Thessalonians, less than twenty years after the death of Christ.

The Christian communities that produced the New Testament, for the most part saw themselves as eschatological communities. They were living the last days. They stood on tip-toe; they were breathless with expectancy. Their attitude was summed up in an acclamation which they did not even take the time to translate from the Aramaic: *Moranatha* O Lord, come (I Cor 16:22)!

The strength of this yearning affected how they lived, worked and prayed. The Our Father is a formulation of their eschatological hope which they had received from Jesus himself. Of course, over emphasis on future hope bears the same dangers as had accompanied the Old Testament Day of the Lord. Some in the New Testament community decided that working for a living was not worth the effort if it was all going to come to an end in a little while anyway. The community was in danger of becoming a hive of busy bodies and drones. Paul has a very simple solution: if they don't work, they don't eat (2 Thes 3:11).

Another danger in the expectation of the *parousia*, is that the description of the last days is usually in terms of apocalyptic. This is a literary form employed in times of crisis which uses language that is meant to frighten and startle, to awaken people from self-complancency. Strange creatures, animals, angels with trumpets and swords abound. These, however, are merely stage props, not to be take literally. But too many, realizing that the description is not to be taken seriously, also do not take the event, the *parousia*, seriously. They leave it for the lunatic fringe who periodically announce the date of the end of the world, and set up housekeeping in the California desert.

The emphasis in the new liturgy has refocused the central place of the *parousia* and eschatology. "As we wait in joyful hope for the coming of our savior Jesus Christ." Such emphasis highlights the Christian tension in our lives that keeps us aware that we have not yet arrived, we are on the way, we are pilgrims. It keeps us breathless in anticipation of the coming of the Kingdom.

Without it, the Church community and the individual tend to think of themselves as being in a state of perfection, with no further growth necessary. We take on the posture of triumphalism, because there is nothing to wait for. We are the Church triumphant. It creates a false impression by hiding the tension that is part of the Gospel.

If ignoring *parousia* and eschatology was commonplace in the past, the pendulum may be swinging too far in the opposite direction today. Perfectionism can be a heresy. With everyone looking for the magic formula to bring about the ideal community, now with the demand for perfect leaders and superiors, now we may be looking for something the Gospel does not promise us.

24.

AS WE WAIT
IN JOYFUL HOPE

The prophets were men that were sent to preach in hopeless times. With their constant denunciations and condemnations, they give the impression of being grim, sour individuals. Poor Jeremiah even lent his name to our English word jeremiad, a weepy, whining lament.

Ezekiel found himself with the thankless task of being sent to a people whom he knew would not listen to him.

Hard of face and obstinate of heart are they to whom I am sending you. But you shall say to them: Thus says the Lord God! And whether they heed or resist — for they are a rebellious house — they shall know that a prophet has been among them. But as for you, son of man, fear neither them nor their words when they contradict you and reject you, and when you sit on scorpions (Ez 2:4-6a).

That's a great way to start out in one's vocation. No wonder some later critics have thought that Ezekiel's writings manifest a bit of neurosis, if not psychosis!

And yet both Jeremiah and Ezekiel, like all the prophets are men of hope. The ground of their hope, however lies neither in their own times, nor in their contemporaries. They know the future will be better, not because the present generation will make it better, but because God never gives up. Jeremiah speaks

159

of a new covenant (31:31) and Ezekiel speaks of a
new heart and a new spirit (37:26). But this is the
work of God who can no more forget his people than
a mother can forget her child.

"Thus says the Lord: cease your cries of mourning,
wipe the tears from your eyes . . . There is hope for
your future, says the Lord . . . Is Ephraim not my
favored son, the child in whom I delight? Often as I
threaten him, I still remember him with favor; my
heart stirs for him, I must show him mercy, says the
Lord (Jer 31:16,17,20). The Hebrew is intensive: I *must*
show him mercy, love, almost as if there is a com-
pulsion with no alternative. Faced with the fickleness
of men, the prophets place their hope in the eternal
love and undying fidelity of Yahweh.

They did not have a preview of coming attractions
to describe the future. Their messianic hope is founded
on the sure conviction that Yahweh will live up to
his name, 'He who is' always with us. Without them,
and the men who gathered around them, sparked to
hope by their word, the Old Testament would be a
dreary picture indeed. It takes a prophet to pierce
the turmoil of the present and grasp on to the God of
enduring love. It takes a prophet to ponder the chaos
and see in it the possibilities for the creative finger
of God.

Their words fell on deaf ears for the most part, but
were preserved in communities of hope. Jesus used
their words to inspire hope in the despairing disciples
on the road to Emmaus (Lk 24:27). In the midst of
his own agony and abandonment, Jesus appeared to
have given up hope. "My God, my God, why have

you forsaken me" (Mk 15:34)? But this is just the opening verse of a psalm he seems to have been praying. It continues, "For he has not spurned nor disdained the wretched man in his misery. Nor did he turn his face away from him, but when he cried out to him, he heard him." And concludes: "And to him my soul shall live; my descendents shall serve him. Let the coming generation be told of the Lord that they may proclaim to a people yet to be born the justice he has shown" (Ps 22:25,31).

After the Resurrection, he appears to the despairing, dejected group in the upper room, and establishes them in hope. His Church is to be a community of hope, because of the fidelity of the God who calls, and also because of the presence of that God within them.

On the evening of that first day of the week, even though the disciples had locked the doors of the place where they were for fear of the Jews, Jesus came and stood before them. "Peace be with you," he said. When he had said this, he showed them his hands and his side. At the sight of the Lord the disciples rejoiced. "Peace be with you," he said again. "As the Father has sent me, so I send you." Then he breathed on them and said: "Receive the Holy Spirit" (Jn 20:19-22).

They will never be alone again, so there is no reason to lose hope.

No matter what would happen to the new-born community, either from enemies without, or dissension within, their hope would be a characteristic that would distinguish them from other men. From prison where he is aware of some in the community who are acting from motives of envy and rivalry, Paul can still write:

What of it? All that matters is that in any and every way, whether from specious motives or genuine ones, Christ is being proclaimed! That is what brings me joy. Indeed, I shall continue to rejoice, in the conviction that this will turn out to my salvation, thanks to your prayers and the support I receive from the Spirit of Jesus Christ. I firmly trust and anticipate that I shall never be put to shame for my hopes; I have full confidence that now as always Christ will be exalted through me, whether I live or die (Phil 1:18-20).

Paul never let the turmoil around him cloud over his hope. He is constantly aware that his strength is "the support I receive from the Spirit of Jesus Christ." All might be in chaos around him but within is hope and joy because of Jesus' gift. "We even boast of our afflictions! We know that affliction makes for endurance and endurance for tested virtue, and tested virtue for hope. And this hope will not leave us disappointed, because the love of God has been poured out in our hearts through the Holy Spirit who has been given to us" (Rom 5:3-5).

He speaks in the plural—us. The Spirit not only comes to the individual, but brings him into community, into the Church. The Greek word for church, *ekklesia* means "to call out from." The Spirit calls us to come out from our loneliness, isolation and despair, and calls us together. Thus hope arises not only from the fact that the Spirit is within us, but he is within the Church and every local manifestation of it.

For my part, from the time I first heard of your faith in the Lord Jesus and your love for all the members of the church, I have never stopped thanking God for you and recommending you in my prayers. May the God of our Lord Jesus Christ, the Father of glory, grant you a spirit of wisdom and insight to know him clearly. May he enlighten your innermost vision that you may know the great hope to which he has called you, the wealth of his glorious heritage to be distributed among the members of the church, and the immeasurable scope of his power in us who believe. It is like the strength he showed in raising Christ from the dead and seating him at his right hand in heaven (Eph 1:15-20).

In trying to describe this power in us and in the community, Paul, with great imagination borrowed two words in common usage, *arrabon* and *sphragis*. "God is the one who firmly establishes us along with you in Christ; it is he who annointed us, and has sealed us (*sphragis*) thereby depositing the first payment (*arrabon*) the spirit, in our hearts" (2 Thes 1:21-22 cf. also Eph 1:14).

The *sphragis* was the seal that a man used on an object to indicate its ownership. It could belong to no other, and no other could make a claim on it. It was also the stamp used by tax accessors (as on a pack of cigarettes today) to indicate that all demands had been satisfied and that the object was in total possession of the owner. Paul says this is what the Holy Spirit is for us. He is the seal, showing to whom we belong, setting us apart so that no other force or power can gain control of us.

He is also the *arrabon*, the down-payment, or pledge. This is easy enough to understand from the practice of buying on the installment plan. When the down

payment is made, although the article is not yet in
full possession of the one who is buying it, neither
can anyone else get hold of it. By his down payment
he has established that one day he will take full possession of it. Thus the Holy Spirit is the Father's
seal and down payment in us. No one else can get
hold of us. His presence is the Father's guarantee
that one day he will take full possession of us. "If
God is for us, who can be against us" (Rom 8:32)?

Many communities today are becoming more Biblical
than they ever thought of becoming. They have gen-
erated their own exodus as many members leave. Those
coming in are few. Established apostolates are falter-
ing or at least being questioned. Structures and regulations which seemed just a few years ago to be of the
very essence of religious life have been criticized and
spurned. Freedom is the cry, but often the necessary
maturity seems to be lacking.

Desperate? Hopeless? Only for those who have forgotten who is in charge, and who it is that calls us
and dwells in us. It is his work not ours, and that
should give us every reason for joy and hope to witness in a world that is so frequently, joyless, hopeless
and desperate.

The faces of the angels on the portals of the medieval gothic cathedral often bear a curious smile, as
if to say "We've got a secret, we know something you
don't know." So do we.

For I am certain that neither death nor life, neither angels
nor principalities, neither the present nor the future, nor powers,
neither height nor depth nor any other creature, will be able

to separate us from the love of God that comes to us in Christ Jesus, our Lord (Rom 8:38,39).

I am writing this in Rome where I recently had a conversation with a Persian woman who is Mohammedan. She said she could never become a Christian, because of the hopeless, joyless expressions that she saw on the faces of so many religious. She wanted to know what kind of a religion could cause people to look so sad.

Who else will be signs of hope, if not religious? Where else can people look for hope and joy, if not in religious communities? Who else has more of a reason to smile?

I plead with you, then, as a prisoner for the Lord, to live a life worthy of the calling you have received, with perfect humility, meekness, and patience, bearing with one another lovingly. Make every effort to preserve the unity which has the Spirit as its origin and peace as its binding force. There is but one body and one Spirit, just as there is but one hope given all of you by your call. There is one Lord, one faith, one baptism; one God and Father of all, who is over all, and works through all, and is in all (Eph 4:1-6).